WAKING DREAM THERAPY
Dream Process as Imagination

Gerald Epstein, M.D.
*Mt. Sinai Hospital and
School of Medicine
New York, New York*

HUMAN SCIENCES PRESS
72 Fifth Avenue   3 Henrietta Street
NEW YORK, NY 10011 ● LONDON, WC2E 8LU

Copyright © 1981 by Human Sciences Press, Inc.
72 Fifth Avenue, New York, New York 10011

All rights reserved. No part of this work may be reproduced or utilized in any form or by any means, electronic or mechanical, including photocopying, microfilm and recording, or by any information storage and retrieval system without permission in writing from the publisher.

Printed in the United States of America
123456789   987654321

Library of Congress Cataloging in Publication Data

Epstein, Gerald, 1935–
   Waking dream therapy.

   Bibliography: p. 223
   Includes index.
    1. Imagination—Therapeutic use. 2. Imagery (Psychology)—Therapeutic use. 3. Psychotherapy. I. Title.
RC489.F35E64   616.89'14   LC80-25925
ISBN 0-89885-018-5

For my mother Celia, Perle, and Colette

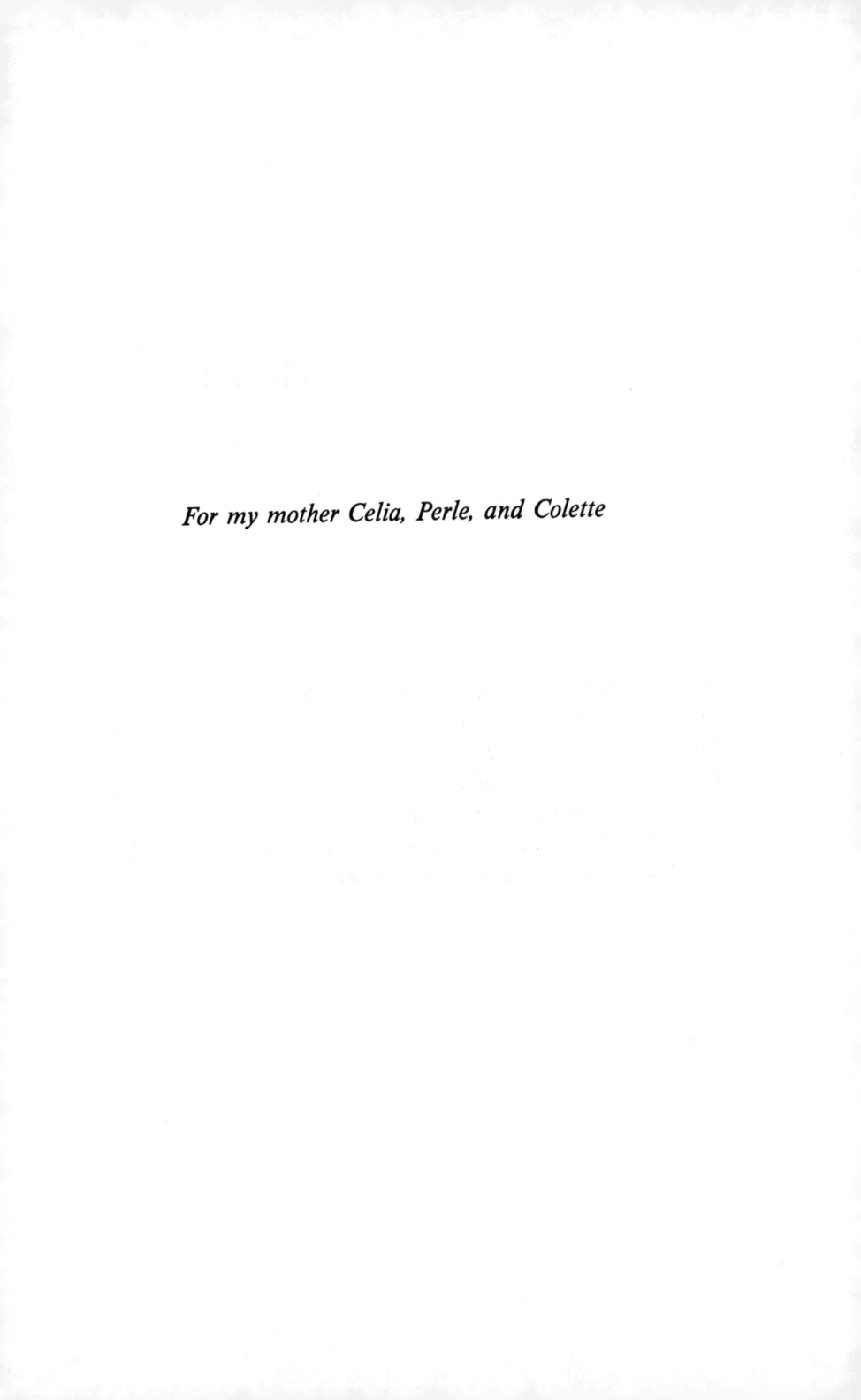

FIGURES

Fig. 1.1 Balance of the realms of reality   29
Fig. 2.1 Hologram (Lensless Photography)   48
Fig. 3.1 Waking Dream Notebook   72
Fig. 5.1 Movement of will   148
Fig. 7.1 Habitual Relationship   189
Fig. E.1 Balancing therapeutic approaches   211
Fig. E.2 The Holomovement. World within
          Worlds.   213

CONTENTS

Preface   9

1. INTRODUCTION   11
    The appreciation of imagination throughout the world
    The framing of a new therapy modality based on imagination called Waking Dream

2. BACKGROUND   38
    The historical place of imagination in Eastern and Western life
    Current scientific directions supporting the validity of imagination

3. JOURNEYING   62
    How to do Waking Dream
    A clinical example

4. ILLUSTRATIONS 98
A sampler of clinical illustrations of Waking Dream Therapy
Waking Dream as a phenomenological therapy

5. PRINCIPLES FOR UNDERSTANDING 147
The philosophical basis for Waking Dream Therapy
The phenomenology of imagination

6. SYMBOLISM 160
A fresh look at symbolism
The integration of symbolism into imaginal life

7. THE THERAPEUTIC RELATIONSHIP 179
Some innovations in conducting therapy
Changing the course of the therapeutic relationship

8. CONTINUING 201
Outlining the fundamental ideas emerging from the phenomenology of Waking Dream Therapy
The relationship of imagination to medicine

EPILOGUE: NOTES ON THE PHENOMENOLOGICAL MODE 211
Summing up phenomenological therapy: ten major points

References 223

Index 229

PREFACE

This book is the beginning explication of a treatment process that I call *waking dream therapy*. The entire method represents a radical departure from most currently employed methods of treatment for human suffering. At the same time, it reintroduces modes of therapy known to the Western world prior to the advent of technological and natural science. The method employs three essential elements: (1) waking dream proper, including the use of guided exercises (to which the current book addresses itself); (2) life plan; and (3) reversing. Each element requires a book of its own; taken together an approach to therapy is formulated that produces lasting transformations of thinking, feeling, and behavior, occurring within a relatively short period of time, giving the recipient hope and joy about the possibilities that exist for fulfillment in this life. The method is not wed to theory or explanation, however, and therefore invites expansions, enlargements, and the touch of each individual practitioner's unique experience.

I hope that I can share my journey with you through these pages, bearing in mind that all cannot be said, captured, nor completely conveyed in written form.

I wish to acknowledge the invaluable editorial and typing assistance of Caroline Suen Shookhoff; and my wife, Perle Epstein, who helped to put the final touches on the book.

G.E.
New York, 1981

Chapter 1

INTRODUCTION

> You meet the nicest people in your dreams.
> Thomas J. (Fats) Waller, 1939

The great event of western psychology in this century took place in 1900 when Freud published *The Interpretation of Dreams*. He attempted to demonstrate that the dream has a significant relationship in the chain of mental life within an individual's experience. This was part of his overall approach, which set out to explain the nature of human mental functioning and to unearth why we behave as we do. Since then much elaboration of Freud's formulation has taken place within the psychodynamic tradition, whose efficacy relies on the primacy of the spoken word and the contents of consciousness (linear thought) strung together by spoken words as the key to unlocking the mysteries of our emotional life.

After an absence of some 300 years imagination is being reintroduced into western therapeutics. This is the next great event for western psychology in this century. The stimulus for this movement has been the discoveries of those functions connected with the activity of the right cerebral hemisphere of the brain, elaborated quite admirably by neurological researchers like Sperry (1973), Gazzinga (1965,1977), and Bogen (1969) among others. They discovered the presence of discrete activity in patients whose corpus callosum had been severed, leaving the two cerebral hemispheres unconnected by the intercalating and interconnecting channels that normally characterize the anatomy of an intact brain. It was noted that the right cerebral hemisphere in these patients operated independently of the left cerebral hemisphere in consistently characteristic ways that suggested that this hemisphere mediates visual events for the human organism. David Galin succinctly summarized these findings in 1974. He indicated that the two cerebral hemispheres perform separate cognitive functions, and when they are surgically disconnected, they operate, as he put it, as "two separate conscious minds in one head . . . they are different not duplicate minds (because of their specialized functions)" (p. 572).

Putting aside the metaphysical question of locating the mind in the head, the service that Galin performs is to bring some respectability and necessary attention to the visual function as an event important in its own right; and to point out that visual perception may operate according to its own laws, which differ from those that pertain to linear logic. With this in mind, I shall attempt in this book to establish imagination as an essential link in the chain of mental life that can help to enrich our physical, emotional, and spiritual life, and I shall introduce a process called *waking dream* for gaining access to this imaginative life.

Both imagination and waking dream need to be defined since western culture disbelieves in the former's reality and is ignorant of the latter's function. Imagination, in common western usage, means the formation of a mental image which is neither real nor present. It is often used synonymously with fantasy, a function similarly perceived as having little to do with the "real" world.

But this has not always been the case. Carol McMahon (1976) illustrated how imagination served a very real function in western life in general and western medicine in particular, which had been holistic prior to the advent of dualistic Cartesian thought in the 17th century. McMahon writes:

> Among the faculties of the soul were sensation, reason, digestion, and imagination. The lattermost was a major theoretical variable in human physiopathology. The theory of imagination-produced disease reached its zenith in Renaissance medical treatises, where its implications for diagnosis, prognostication and therapy were fully elaborated. Although the conceptualization of imagination as causal in altering bodily functions antedated Aristotle, it was his formulation which became the received view of the Renaissance. (p. 179)
>
> It was this soul which accounts for the historical greatness of psychological medicine. When Descartes (1596–1650) redefined soul as "immaterial substance" or "mind," imagination's role in the disease process was irrevocably taken from it. An era ensued in which the existence of "mental illness" was denied. How, it was asked, could an "immaterial substance" possibly be sick?
>
> We have failed to profit from the accomplishments of our early predecessors because of a discontinuity in the history of medicine. In the pre-Cartesian era, medicine was invariably holistic or psychosomatic. In the post-Cartesian dualistic era, mechanistic physiopathology gained ascendancy, and psychophysiological events were forbidden on logical grounds. (p. 183–184)

Before Descartes, imagination was thought to reside in the ventricles of the brain and to be the regulator of visual phenomena, which encompassed dreams and hallucinations as well as emotions. The individual who was treated for physical and emotional disorders was given exercises that involved his visualizing capacity. An object might appear to the individual during these exercises. In waking life, the individual would then acquire such an object to wear as a talisman or amulet, to remind him of the discoveries he made about himself and his disturbance by using his imagination. He was thereby able to sustain the influence of imagination in his everyday life and live this continuity between the imaginal and waking life.

It is interesting that imagination was located in the brain. Current investigation of right hemispheric activity has accorded this hemisphere of the brain the function of mediating activity of the imagination. This is a *nonrational* thought process dealing with gestaltic perception. Significantly, the right cerebral hemisphere is connected with functions of the left side of the body, which is the location of the heart. Numerous cultures, including the Hebraic and ancient Egyptian (Schwaller de Lubicz, 1977) and the North American Indian (Séjourné, 1967) call imagination and holistic perception the "intelligence of the heart." Our medieval and Renaissance ancestors as well seemed to have had an intuitive awareness of the meaningfulness of the imaginative function which connects the heart with the brain.

In numerous nonwestern cultures, imagination has always been, and remains still, accepted as a very real function. Henry Corbin (1972), one of the leading western scholars of Islamic thought, writes:

> In other words, if in French (and in English) usage we equate the *imaginary* [author's emphasis] with the unreal, the utopian, this is undoubtedly symptomatic of something that contrasts with an order of reality which I call the *mundus imaginalis,* and which the theosophers of Islam designate as the "eighth clime." After a brief outline of *this order of reality* [my emphasis], we shall discuss the organ which perceives it, i.e., imaginative consciousness, *cognitive Imagination* [my emphasis]. . . . (p. 2)

Further he writes:

> . . . the world of the image, the *mundus imaginalis:* a world that is ontologically as real as the world of the senses and that of the

intellect. This world requires its own faculty of perception, namely, imaginative power, a faculty with a cognitive function, a *noetic* [author's emphasis] value which is as real as that of sense perception or intellectual intuition. (p. 7)

H. H. Price (1965), an English philosopher, elegantly affirms the real existence of the imaginal world:

... Paradoxical as it may sound there is nothing imaginary about a mental image. It is an actual entity, as real as anything can be. The seeming paradox arises from the ambiguity of the verb "to imagine." It does sometimes mean "to have mental images." But more usually it means "to entertain propositions without believing them"; and very often they are false propositions, and moreover we disbelieve them in the act of entertaining them. This is what happens, for example, when we read Shakespeare's play *The Tempest,* and that is why we say Prospero and Ariel are "imaginary characters." Mental images are not in this sense imaginary at all. We do actually experience them, and they are no more imaginary than sensations. To avoid the paradox, though at the cost of some pedantry, it would be well to distinguish between imagining and imaging, and to have two different adjectives "imaginary" and "imagy".... Indeed, to those who experienced it an image-world would be just as "real" as the present world is ... (pp. 4–5)

In connection with the ontologically real world of image described by Corbin, and with the organ of perception, i.e., cognitive imagination or imaginative power, I am here introducing a treatment technique connected with imaginative power called *waking dream therapy.* Waking dream, as the manifestation and instrument for imagination in psychotherapy, has had, and still has numerous proponents, stemming back to the earliest days of this century in Europe and into America in the present day.

Waking dream is still a term commonly used by practitioners of imagery techniques. One example is a recent book by Mary Watkins entitled *Waking Dreams* (1976). We also find the term used by writers and poets. In Keats's *Ode to a Nightin-*

gale we find the line: "Was it a vision or a waking dream?" The Irish writer George Russell (who wrote under the pseudonym AE) describes very well the waking dream experiences that influenced and shaped his life in his book *Candle of Vision* (1965). William Blake wrote extensively about the veracity of the imagination:

> This world of Imagination is the world of Eternity; it is the divine bosom into which we shall all go after the death of the Vegetated body. This World of Imagination is Infinite & Eternal, whereas the world of Generation, or Vegetation, is Finite & Temporal. There Exist in that Eternal World the Permanent Realities of Every Thing which we see reflected in this Vegetable Glass of Nature. All Things are comprehended in their Eternal Forms in the divine body of the Saviour, the True Vine of Eternity, The Human Imagination . . . (1810) (p 605)

Keats (1952) also wrote eloquently of the imagination:

> I am certain of nothing but of the holiness of the Heart's Affections and the truth of Imagination—what the imagination seizes as Beauty must be truth—whether it existed before or not—for I have the same Idea of all our Passions as of Love they are all in their sublime, creative of Essential Beauty. (p. 67)

Visual phenomena like night dreams and waking dreams are concrete manifestations of a movement of energy that flows through abstract intellection to concrete sensory experiences. Hence, *all* visual phenomena are revelatory and need to be translated into statements about existence that include options available for fulfillment; avenues or possibilities closed off from fulfillment; and pointers toward the action that must be taken to concretize the fulfillment. The action of waking dream and guided exercise[1] not only permits the seeing of possibilities but also the doing of possibilities, the effects of which are brought back to concrete reality and are actively used to create one's existence.

The function of imagination was put very succinctly and clearly by Rabbi Abraham Isaac Kuk (Agus, 1972):

> The perception of ontological truth is dependent upon the development of the power of imagination, *a special non-rational faculty* ... [my emphasis] (p. 162)

and

> In the treasury of imagination, all truth and greatness are contained; these become manifest little by little through the restrictive, filtering channels of reason. Our rational faculty is but a humble disciple.... All praise is due to the vital force of our higher imagination ... which unites with the higher Reason.
> The Power of imagination is the "chair" on which the light of wisdom and of the higher life rest.... The exalted state of imagination obtains as long as man adheres to the standards of holiness; secular imagination, on the other hand, contains only the reflected power of the shadow (of reason) and is the source of cynicism ... (p. 163).

What does this mean for understanding the imagination and dream experience? Among other things it means that we accept dreams as valid, important in their own right and not necessarily to be judged solely by the standards of waking life. In this way the dream is accorded a position as a realm just as real as waking life. Therefore, we can replace the oft used phrase, "last night I had a dream, but in *reality* ..." by "last night I had a dream but in *waking life* ..." Further, we can immediately drop the ideas of latent and manifest dream. These ideas are a product of many speculative presuppositions, among which is that the dream has no meaning by itself, but acquires meaning only when the "life" of concrete reality through the agency of associational thought is breathed into it. This latter action immediately devalues and renders inauthentic an integral part of human existence. By accepting the dream as real, one is directed to look at what the dream reveals about us *in its own language,* a language that is analogical, concrete, nonlinear, and directly representational. Dreams can be seen as a sign function that reveals something about oneself, as well as events that may take place subsequently; or they may indicate corrective actions to take or confirmations of one's behavior.

Ordinarily in clinical work, the dream is used as a stimulus for associations and as a subject for analysis. But this is not the only possibility. The dream can also be *explored* as waking life is explored. The essential action of waking dream is the patient's *imagining* himself to be in the dream and *continuing* its movement in a *waking state.* This action reveals possibilities for living that if followed through, can help free us from the restrictions we habitually live with in the concrete world. We recognize the meaningfulness of what addresses us from out there in ways not previously available, which helps us to know what action is appropriate to be carried out in the concrete world.

In a related way, waking dream takes into account the expression of emotion. From the perspective of phenomenology, images are the concretizations of emotions. Therefore, the exploration of the imaginal realm is in effect the immersing of oneself into emotion. This is in fact what is meant by "the intelligence of the heart."

By accepting these existences as real, we can begin to accept and appreciate *all* aspects of human experience as real without elevating one mode as more real than another: we no longer assume, then, that linear logical thought is the only framework within which all human activity should be translated. On the contrary, we find that in the imaginal existence, we are able to *see* with a vision not limited by the ordinary time-space parameters of concrete reality. This seeing allows us to "get outside" of the personal self and thus see our existence from a different, nonhabitual vantage point. What is seen brings with it knowledge about the individual's relationship to the concrete world and to his own biological being, a knowledge that is unshakeable and that can be used in everyday life.

Rather than introduce a new term, I am seeking to show

how my use of waking dream differs from any of the current usages of imagery in western culture. I owe my insights to my own discoveries under the teaching of Mme. Colette Aboulker-Muscat of Jerusalem. It was she who first showed me what was possible in imaginal realms, and then encouraged me to discover what I could do by myself. Her example as well as my own explorations taught me what I believe to be the deep truths about participating in genuine psychotherapy. Mme. Muscat's own understanding is an outgrowth of her work as a student of Robert Desoille, modified by her vast clinical experience of over 30 years.

Simply put, waking dream is the carrying out of dream life in the waking state along two distinct lines. The first is that the "patient" continue his night dream in the session and explore the elements that constitute the dream setting or action by describing to the "therapist"[2] his existence as he now experiences it. For this exploration to take place, optimally, the patient should place himself in the dream by first relaxing with his eyes closed and with noise levels diminished so that external reality is sealed out as much as possible. Following this phase, called the induction, the patient is asked to imagine himself back in the dream at the point which the patient considers to be most significant. He is then asked to describe what is seen, heard, and felt, as well as any other sensory experiences that might occur. He will then begin to explore and describe the dream existence, finding himself moving rather quickly out of that domain into a region that is ontologically real, experienced as such, but, like the dream reality, not governed by the laws that apply to the world of concrete waking life. It is in this realm that the individual literally sees possibilities for his existence as well as the way to fulfill those possibilities; he might also apprehend those possibilities that can be but have not yet been capable of fulfillment. If the apprehended way is available, he then moves to fulfill that possibility through some action in that realm.

This action is closely associated with the second line of

waking dream work, that of living the function of waking dream in the world of concrete reality (or waking life). This means that the journeyer needs to carry out in the physical action of waking life the possibility fulfilled in the imaginal realm. Waking dream allows us to move beyond the confines of physical reality, which is governed by its own particular laws of causality, to another realm of perceptual reality, where physically derived notions of time and space do not apply. In this, waking dream is similar to another realm of perceptual reality, namely, one's dream life, which is not governed by the waking life standards of time and space.

In stating that one must allow the imaginal to inform waking life, I am taking a stance that may be controversial but one that at the same time offers a new perspective on a problem that has dogged psychology over the course of this century. The premise is that physical man—the "I think therefore I am" man—is not the center from which experience is produced. Instead he is a vehicle for the manifestation of experience, in which man and what is encountered exist as a unit; the occurrence of this unit constitutes what is known as experience. There are two realities, then, which meet in experience: man and that which man meets. Therefore, what one meets is not a "projection," in the psychological sense, of one's "psyche," that is, it is not produced or created by man. This means that whatever is encountered is real. What is left to man thereafter is the freedom to interpret the experience as unreal. It is here that one "projects" one's subjective notions onto life events. What is posited is that man can exist simultaneously in many orders of reality, which are different from the order of the substantial world. These orders or worlds cannot be apprehended by intellectual or rational thought processes, and in fact, demand that we bypass rational thought in order to know them. It is further posited that what can be gleaned by linear logical thought processes does not constitute the totality of man. The stance goes even further to maintain that human life is characterized by the existence both *here*—in the sense of a physical corporeality which is lived through rational thought expressed by sequentially ordered language—and *there*—in the sense that we transcend the limits of physical dimension (weight, volume, mass, location) imposed on all concrete objects. The *here* existence is concerned with quantity while the *there* existence is concerned with quality. It is only by transcending physicality, as we do in waking dream, that we can learn how to balance the quantitative and qualitative existences.

By focusing only on the rational aspects of the individual "I," western society perceives the self as fixed or static and rejects the dialectical nature of self that is both fixed and flowing, and thus constantly changing. Because of the predilection which seeks a solution outside the dialectic, neither natural nor current physiological science can unravel the primary problem of modern western psychology, that of *narcissism*.

We often call schizophrenics "narcissistic." Here narcissism means a preoccupation with the personal self not in terms of self-love but rather in terms of self-hate.[3] These patients do not love but loathe themselves. This loathing arises because they are less able than most people to experience the cessation of their existence, to move from the quantitative to the qualitative, and from there to fulfill the possibilities of their existence. They are unable to act in the concrete world and this paralysis contributes to their fragmentation and withdrawal from the world. Their inability to move disgusts them, leaving them feeling hatred, mistrust, and fear toward themselves and everything around them.

We recognize that the answer to narcissism lies in experiencing the cessation of the excessive pull toward personal self interest in waking life. That physical man must grapple with the cessation of the physicality that is his very nature is difficult, to say the least. But waking dream suggests that we can actively harmonize our quantitative and qualitative selves, a possibility virtually untouched by rational thought processes. This harmony generates a sense of relief from the preoccupation with our physical being.

The act of motion unavailable to many schizophrenics is vitally important to the realization of potential in all of us. Motion permits us to translate qualitative possibilities into quantitative carrying out, i.e., into physicality. It is this carrying out that permits us to open ourselves to what exists beyond the physical sphere. If we fail to carry out those possibilities, we fall behind, or fall into debt, as it were, to ourselves. From there on, feelings of guilt and inhibition take over, leading to paralysis of action. We then must come to rely more heavily on thought, at the expense of lived experience, to help us fulfill our lives.

Because linear thought does not contain the potential for action it cannot help us fulfill our possibilities. Linear thought by its very nature can only reflect the past. The future on the other hand is by *definition* potential and nonexistent. By trying to apply linear thought to the future, we can only become more and more fragmented, since we are always applying the past to our experience and removing ourselves from the present moment at the same time. The future, from my perspective, is transformed into the present by its fulfillment through our physical presence and physical action in the world of concrete reality. It is cyclical because the newly transformed present simultaneously generates a new potential, a new future.[4] Here we see how the nonmaterial world influences the material.

Let me illustrate this more concretely. The physical carrying out of a possibility involves three distinct acts: perceiving, apprehending, moving. First, there is the perceiving (seeing) of the possibility. This seeing may be linked to primary insight and implies that at the outset the perceiver is one with the perceived and *understands in that perception the inherent meaning of the perceived.* (For example, calling a tree by name means that the general class "tree" is understood since otherwise no single tree could be distinguished as such—our perceiving goes from the general to the particular, as the gestaltists have indicated, rather than the other way around.) Schematically speaking, the act of perceiving is followed by the apprehending of a way to fulfill that perceptual possibility. This apprehending is followed by the movement toward or away from its fulfillment. It is only in this third phase, and not before, that we know, i.e., sense, our physical being. The second phase is thought, but thought used appropriately to tell us *how* to fulfill a goal. What to do and when to do is not a proper subject for thought and is part of the third phase only, the phase of action. I *see* a friend ahead of me on the street; I *decide* to run to catch up with him; then I *run*. In running I become aware of my physical nature. If I do not run I am still aware of my physical nature, which at that moment is associated with not running. If I see, apprehend, and do not act, I might be in debt to what has called upon me to fulfill itself. If I do not apprehend a way to do so, I am made aware of the limitations of my human existence. These limitations I can either accept, or once realizing their existence, can try to overcome. It is here that one can move back into the form of waking dream work I call *guided exercises* to seek an active way to complete the action called forth by what is perceived.

Besides the voyage itself into the imaginal world and the living of the imaginal world in waking life, two other aspects of waking dream to mention at this point are: the return journey from the waking dream voyage and the role of the therapist in this work. The traveller returns from his excursion into the imaginal realm along the same route he used in the going. Going and returning along the same route is consonant with the original precedent for journeying set by the patriarch Abraham, who travelled from Chaldea throughout the Near East to Egypt and back again by *the same route*. As he returned he paid homage to those he had met along the way and paid back debts to those from whom he had borrowed on the trip. And perhaps he returned with a new perception about the things he passed on his original journey.

The therapist in waking dream therapy acts both as an *instructor* and an *advisor* who can give directions to the explorer in this new spatial terrain, which is unfamiliar and surprising. I shall flesh out these two new dimensions for the therapist in greater detail later on, but let me note here that in conducting this work, the therapist as instructor and advisor *must refrain from:* interpreting events either during or after the waking dream, imposing on the person's freedom to learn for himself, allowing either himself or the patient to "free associate" during or after the work. The instructor does provide specific instruction before, during, and after waking dream, which can be characterized as giving intention (before), direction (during), and continuity (after) in that order.

Neither Freud nor Jung was a stranger to visual imagery. For Jung, active imagination became a technique that he used commonly in his therapeutic work although he did not write this up in a systematic way. He began with the patient's night dream, usually starting where the dream ended, but it is unclear whether Jung or the patient decided that this was the most significant point. Jung also offered a good deal of interpretation about the phenomena encountered, which I believe counters the overall benefits that the use of visual imagination can provide.

Rix Weaver attempts to organize and present coherently the clinical application of active imagination in her book *The Old Wise Woman* (1973). In this work, she links the phenomenon of active imagination to the *theoretical* notions of Jungian thought and in her own work interprets a good deal of the patient's experience. I shall discuss later on my objection to linking waking dream to *any* interpretation or clinical explanation.

Freud was aware of the presence of imagery. He would elicit visual scenes from his patients by touching their foreheads until, toward the end of the 19th century, he decided that psychoanalytic method should deal solely with the realm of linear thought. He apparently went through some sort of transitional phase from touching to talking via visual imagery, for he describes a "waking dream" experience he conducted with a 14-year-old boy in 1899. This case, which he believed had a successful resolution, is the only waking dream experience discussed in any of his writings.

The case is as follows: (Vol. V, pp. 618–619)

A fourteen-year-old boy came to me for psycho-analytic treatment suffering from *tic convulsif,* hysterical vomiting, headaches, etc. I began the treatment by assuring him that if he shut his eyes he would see pictures or have ideas, which he was then to communicate to me. He replied in pictures. His last impression before coming to me was revived visually in his memory. He had been playing at draughts with his uncle and saw the board in front of him. He thought of various positions, favourable or unfavourable, and of moves that one must not make. He then saw a dagger lying on the board—an object that belonged to his father but which his imagination placed on the board. Then there was a sickle lying on the board and next a scythe. And there now appeared a picture of an old peasant mowing the grass in front of the patient's distant home with a scythe. After a few days I discovered the meaning of this series of pictures. The boy had been upset by an unhappy family situation. He had a father who was a hard man, liable to fits of rage, who had been unhappily married to the patient's mother, and whose educational methods had consisted of threats. His father had been divorced from his mother, a tender and affectionate woman, had married again and had one day brought a young woman home with him who was to be the boy's new mother. It was during the first few days after this that the fourteen-year-old boy's illness had come on. His suppressed rage against his father was what had constructed this series of pictures with their understandable allusions. The material for them was provided by a recollection from mythology. The sickle was the one with which Zeus castrated his father; the scythe and the picture of the old peasant represented Kronos, the violent old man who devoured his children and on whom Zeus took such unfilial vengeance. His father's marriage gave the boy an opportunity of repaying the reproaches and threats which he had heard from his father long before because he had played with his genitals. (Cf. the playing at draughts; the forbidden moves; the dagger which could be used to kill.) In this case long-repressed memories and derivatives from them which had remained unconscious slipped into consciousness by a roundabout path in the form of apparently meaningless pictures.

With Freud—as indicated in this case description—I raise the same objection as I did with Jung, that of the tendency to interpret the phenomena. Interpretation removes the images from the sphere of their own being and subordinates them to a mode of understanding that is not a synthesizing one—the world of linear thought. The images are not permitted to speak for themselves but are instead subjected to a distortion through intellectualizing. (see below)

Recent investigation by psychologists who have been able to step outside of the limits imposed by the locus of interest of psychology, i.e., cognitive linear thinking, has allowed them to begin to understand the importance of the functions that stand apart from rational inquiry (Ten Houten & Kaplan, 1973). But not all psychologists have been able to accommodate themselves to this new locus of investigation, and therein lies a problem. Joseph Rychlak (1968) has quite clearly stated the general difficulty of psychology:

> Man devised his scientific methods, and he alone can adjust his thinking about how to use them most productively and usefully. *Psychology's problems are at heart the fundamental problems of man's use of intellect* [my emphasis]. Before we can resolve the inner contradictions of the science of psychology we must first revise our thinking about the nature of scientific knowledge. In doing so, we will not depart from our sister sciences, but actually come more into line with them. (p. 3)

Rychlak rightly relates the problems of current psychological investigation to the intellect and to knowing as a function of intellect. This capacity is commonly called *rational process*. What has to be considered in psychologic investigations, however, is the *nonrational* processes. Because of the prejudices within science in general and psychology in particular, these processes have been mistakenly labelled "irrational," the denotation and connotation of this label being "unreal."

Ken Wilber (1977), as well as Ten Houten and Kaplan (1973), have made a valiant attempt to set the record straight. The latter authors point out how psychology by its own tenets can only deal with logical thought processes and cannot, therefore, investigate those processes that they term appositional, or not framed within the propositional framework of syllogistic logic.

In the framework of syllogistic logic or propositional thought, the thought process can be described as rational or irrational or logical or illogical. But those processes mediated by the right cerebral hemisphere cannot be evaluated by a terminology that applies to left hemispheric functioning alone. These processes are also called nondeterministic because they do not exist according to the causal laws and principles which govern linear thought. It is unwarranted, therefore, to call the activity mediated by right hemispheric functioning irrational or illogical. Rather, these processes must be called *nonrational* or *nonlogical.* This adjustment of perception should help erode the stigma of being "unreal" from these functions and allow them to assume their place as a real and meaningful content in the chain of mental life. By relinquishing this prejudice, we can bring these functions into productive harmony with our already existing logical framework.

The function that predominates within a given society depends largely on the social conditioning of that culture.[5] For example, it was reported that prior to World War II, the social organization of the Senoi Indians of the Malay peninsula encouraged and depended on the reporting and understanding of dreams (Stewart, 1969). The dream, a nonlogical, nonlinear movement, was *the* significant shaper of their culture. The Senoi themselves attributed their nonviolent nature and lack of crime, no significant familial disharmony, and no need for a police force to their creative use of dreaming.

This is not to say that we should do away with linear logical thinking and the language it begets. What is being asked, however, is that western man attempt to overcome the effects of a social conditioning that attenuates the harmonizing of hemispheric functioning and so in effect deprives us of one of our greatest freedoms, i.e., the use of imagination.

The introduction of a visual mode into our repertoire can serve to help balance the tendency to rely on words, interpretation, and theorizing, which characterizes western psychotherapy. The aim of imagery work is not to compete with the verbal mode for our attention, but rather to lend impetus to a fundamental principle existing in science—as well as nature—that of harmony, or equilibrium, or unity. While all these terms might not be directly synonymous with each other, they are related to the notion of *balance*. So, it is with the principle of balance in mind that waking dream endeavors to bring the world of the imagination into harmony with the world of the empirical, and to bring the visual mode into harmony with the lexical (Fig. 1.1). These are all aiming toward bringing about a balance of human function consonant with the balance of the function of nature in general. Thus we allow ourselves to realize our unity with nature, present from the outset of our existence on earth, a nature of which we are an integral part, but from which we have been cut off by the miseducation, poor parental rearing, and the imposed functional myths about what is "good" and "right" for us as members of the human community.

The need to clarify the real existence of imaginal events is intrinsically connected with another point of importance: our coming to understand that imaginal phenomena are the language of realms of existence that are genuinely there, although ordinarily inaccessible to us in everyday life.

What is given to a human being at birth is the possibility of living in and as these modes of existence. The realm of existence called waking life is lived via the mode of spoken language as a linear logical thought process, and also via the use of the sense organs in the world of concrete matter. It is when we are able to go behind, as it were, the world lived by the senses in concrete reality that we can know of the existence of other realms, lived via the mode of imaginal thoughts. Henry Corbin (1972) describes this situation very clearly.

> It must be stressed that the world into which those Oriental theosophers probed is perfectly *real* [author's emphasis]. Its reality is more irrefutable and more coherent than that of the

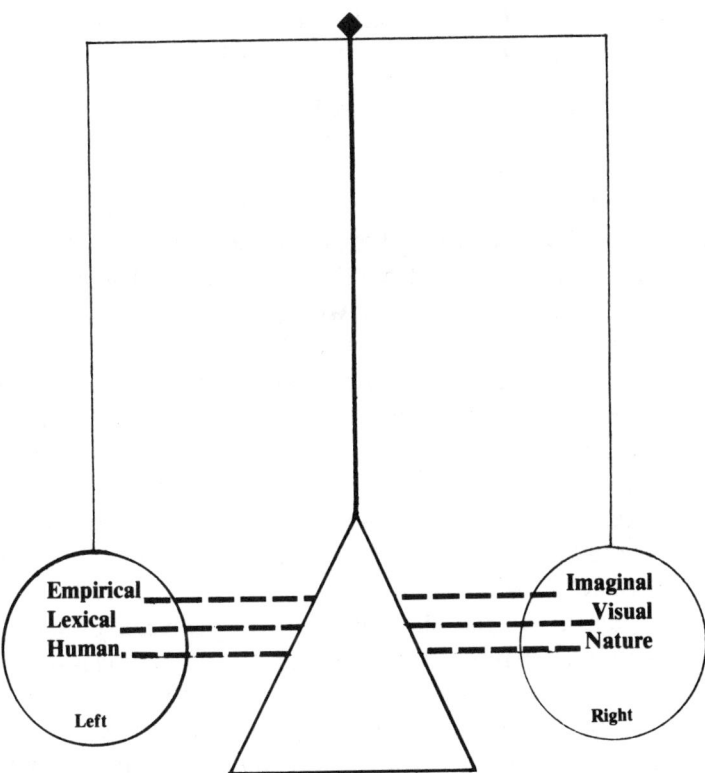

Each realm on the L scale has its counterpart on the R scale. The empirical realm is that of concrete reality matched by a nonmaterial reality called *Imaginal*. We can apprehend either if we choose. The articulation of the empirical happens as lexical while that of the imagination happens as visual (although not entirely). The human realm is causally conditioned and interpretive. Thus, the empirical and lexical realms are causally construed. The nature realm occurs phenomenologically, i.e., without interpretation. Thus, the imaginal and visual realms occur as is, i.e., without interpretation acausally apprehended in the immediacy of the experiential moment.

Figure 1.1 Balance of the realms of reality

> empirical world, where *reality* [author's emphasis] is perceived by the senses. Upon returning, the beholders of this world are perfectly aware of having been "elsewhere"; they are not mere schizophrenics. This world is hidden behind the very act of sense perception and has to be sought underneath its apparent objective certainty. For this reason we definitely cannot qualify it as being *imaginary* [author's emphasis] in the current sense of the word, i.e., as unreal or non-existent. (p. 15)

The implication is that the human being lives in various existences, of which waking life is but one. Another existence is that of the dream, which from the phenomenological perspective, is real and should be acknowledged as such. It is an existence of form but not of substantial matter. There is great malleability and flexibility in dream events. Linear time is not a prominent factor and space becomes easily permeable. Logical sequences are not adhered to, nonetheless beings appear, events occur, and personal experiences, including sensory ones, take place. What is here proposed in relation to the dream can stand as the phenomenological paradigm of the way to look at all experience of whatever nature.[6]

In contrast to the phenomenological perspective, one of the essential elements of standard dream understanding is that it is divided into a "manifest and "latent" content. This belief immediately devaluates the dream phenomenon as it presents itself and contradicts Freud's intention stated at the outset of *The Interpretation of Dreams:* namely that the dream occupies a meaningful place in the activities of the mental life of a human being. By not accepting the dream as a phenomenon of human experience, genuine in its own right as revelatory and expressive of the individual's relationship to life, the dream is not accorded its meaningful place as a realm of human existence. Rather, it is said that the manifest dream is a disguise concealing some supposed latent content. This action, immediately devaluates the phenomenon and deprives it of its reality. Within the phenomenological framework there is no distinction between manifest and latent content; rather, the dream experience is focused upon with the attendant consideration that the dream is a real existence where concrete sensory experiences are met. It is, therefore, neither a disguise for some supposed latent meaning, nor is it a metaphorical comment. It is a revelatory statement, usually visual, about the dreamer's relationship to life. It is not constructed by the dreamer's "psyche" as a visual metaphor (to consider it thus, in my view, leads to obstructive psychological consequences by encouraging the tendency toward narcissism i.e., it becomes something "I make" rather than something we find). The task of the dreamer is to look at the dream from the vantage point of waking life and let the dream disclose what possibilities and potentials for fulfillment are open or closed to him (Boss, 1977).

If we acknowledge this phenomenological principle that reality embraces nonmaterial spatiality and form, we can enlarge the dimensions of human experience which includes accepting the experiences of those we label "aberrant" or "irrational." Recognizing the reality of nonmaterial spatiality and form prompts us to make the shift from the burden of having to sort out the "rational" from the "irrational" to accepting the genuineness and authenticity of all experience, be it substantial or insubstantial.

Given all the contrary habits and indoctrination of our training, both as children and adults, this shift is painful. This new way of looking at the nature of reality does not coincide with currently held views. If the shift is attempted and the pain endured, the reward may well be worth the trouble, because you will allow yourself to see reality in a new light. It will become less necessary to stand outside of another's existence judging the "correctness" of that existence acccording to your own perconceived notions about "reality."

As we are born, so are all existences born. That is the meaning of ontic: that which exists and is real. The universe and the earth constantly create. Human beings create and are created. We can extend ourselves beyond the limits of our physicality to experience other creations. Our self-importance does not allow us to grant ontic status to other creations, however, especially if they are not creations of our own making. Natural science always places man at the center of experience. He makes or produces dreams, fantasies, hallucinations, and the like. How self-centered! We try to dominate all that we survey, be it nature, other people, or spatial realms that we cannot grasp. Given this prejudiced disposition, we cannot grant ontological being to the events that address us from out there, i.e., that are not a "product of our own making."

Only experience can convince us of the truth of an image or event not made by man. Such an event can be viewed as a potential for existence, of which fulfillment in everyday life may or may not take place. (This "taking place in everyday life" is used interchangeably with living, doing, acting, all of which are synonymous with becoming.) It is here that we have to complement the prevalent view of dynamic psychology, which stresses the importance of verbal thought as "trial action" as a key to knowing ourselves, with the view of phenomenological synthesis, which stresses the importance of "actional trying."

The assumption that thought is "trial action" ultimately leads to an emphasis differing from that of waking dream. The "trial action" view of thought leads to the conclusion that thought should precede action in order that "reality testing" be properly developed. It is felt that ultimately this "trial action" will facilitate "appropriate" action based on "reality" considerations. When one adopts this view one is also adopting an entire set of philosophical presuppositions about what constitutes "reality" and "reality testing."[7] Along with this philosophical slant often comes the misapprehension that thought is action or a substitute for action. One of the consequences of the "trial action" idea has been the development of a prejudiced view of the behavior now called "acting out." This term, which, strictly speaking, denotes a clinical phenomenon about the behavior directed toward the therapist but carried out with or toward someone outside of the treatment setting, has always been used pejoratively by clinicians when describing patients' behavior. It is only "natural" in any system that values "trial action" over "acting out" that the spoken word would achieve a preeminence over other modes of expression and would become the yardstick by which human activity would be measured. Anything displacing the centrality of "trial action" would perforce be considered inimical to the therapeutic endeavor. From the perspective of dynamic understanding, there is hardly anything more justified than "trial action," for words are valued as the ore out of which can be shaped a "sensible understanding of our world."

From the phenomenological perspective there is an obstacle posed for understanding in trying to "make sense" of experience, i.e., in finding the causal relatedness between events. In so doing, a promise is held out that our reason can triumph over all the passions and eruptions of impulses, and can harness them for more beneficial use. The phenomenological view holds that our development depends on fulfillment and engagement of those potentials in the concrete world. Here the word *dynamic* takes on its truer meaning, that is, the movement or transformation of something unshaped to that of full shape, as when a block of wood becomes a table. Fulfillment requires the initiation of action, whereas thought as trial action tends toward inhibiting rather than toward advancing appropriate action. The phenomenological position maintains that the proper function of thought—as "trial action" linked to verbal usage—is to determine the "how to do" of experience; but it is inappropriate to determine the "what to do" or "when to do" of experience.

Linear thought cannot provide a basis for experience, especially thought that habitually anticipates outcomes, seeks goals, or knows what to expect, in short, thought related to the future. Because such thought is connected to "things", it is rooted in the past, where there is no newness and no uniqueness. Applying habitual thought to the future is essentially "magical" because it conceives the future as a thing that already exists and is, therefore, capable of being shaped. The future is by definition unknown and a potential without form, however. The notion of future as *thing* to be shaped underlies all talking therapies based on the unfolding of thought causally linked. Linear thought can only grow out of past experiences, which it views in terms of concrete things. It naturally follows that linear thought will similarly conceive the future in terms of things and thereby as being determined only by the past. Such a tendency is "magical" because the future is not a thing and is therefore not subject to apprehension by linear thought. The future as potential is apprehendable only by fulfillment through the actional mode of experience. In a like manner, the act of imagination brings with it an act of discovery.

A psychology of experience can be equated with one of becoming, which is action, experiencing, doing, and living. Our view reverses the notion that thought as "trial action" permits "reality testing" and "relationship to reality" to occur. Experience yields knowledge of reality. Words beget more words but they cannot be translated into experience. Words may be used to describe experience but they are not a substitute for experience. Nor can they analyze or interpret experience (although this is how they are commonly used) without distorting, diluting, and intellectualizing experience.

Abstracting experiences to word forms fails to acknowledge the genuineness of what is encountered. Words used interpretively cannot capture the pure instant of the present moment. Instead, these qualities are transmuted by logic and the desire to "make sense" out of experience. We allow logic to conclude that what is in fact a subjective experience or evaluation is instead seemingly objective. This is an erroneous translation arising from the failure to see that logical thought always grows from a subjective ground. The consequence of this tendency is to concentrate on the movement of the logical process rather than on the immediacy of experience.

Experiential modes, including imaging, are *all* nondeterministic or acausal events. There is no parallel contingency as one finds in cause and effect thinking, where two elements must always be connected or linked by one's influence on the other. The imaginal and dream worlds operate according to their own laws, which do not obtain in the thought operation of the waking world, but rather are acausal. Yet the laws of the waking world, governed by linear thought, are used to account for the existence and meaning of the imaginal and dream worlds, which operate along acausal, nondeterministic lines. This misapplication is scientifically unsound (Schroedinger, 1946) and is misleading, when implicitly imparted to a patient in psychotherapy.

One misapprehension about reality that has ramifications for the treatment of emotional problems is the belief that experience can be translated into linear interpretation. Mistranslation results from the evaluation of behavior by logical criteria where verbal thinking is construed as the cause of action. But what if lexical thought and action are both aspects of an all-embracing relatedness of natural phenomena, each a mode with its own language of expression? Seen this way, each expression would be appreciated in its own right as being a possibility for existing in the world. If we accept that behavior should not be judged solely by logical criteria, then we might be able to overcome our prejudices about what constitutes "normality"—any deviation from which is considered "pathology." At present, psychiatry has established a complete taxonomy that defines aberration as any behavior, relatedness, thought process or mood variation that does not conform to a hypothetical norm, a norm that has never been clearly defined or demonstrated. Our subjective estimation of normality is based on vague impressions and speculations which have been taken for "reality." Once this subjective attitude becomes acknowledged as the only or primary "reality," (as is the case presently in modern psychiatry) then "deviation" from that standard, which is now viewed as "objective" is designated "unreal" or "abnormal."

The business of current "objective psychology" is to attempt to quantify this fundamentally subjective value by translating the subjective appraisal into some "objectively" tangible one. The result of these psychological gyrations is that we have refused to allow experience to stand on its own, but rather, we subject it to what we think about experience. Once we move from experience to "thought about experience," we immediately begin to make value judgments about who is doing what and whether what they are doing is right or wrong.

In sum, experience cannot be grasped through logical thought. The imaginal realm to be outlined in the succeeding pages is a reality when looked at from the perspective of lived experience. This realm is qualitatively not quantitatively spatial. It is not subject to the laws governing temporality. It is not a "projection" created by a material brain out of a hypothetical psyche. *We encounter, seek, and explore this realm in exactly the same way we do the material world: with our five senses.* These other levels of reality in which we live can be discovered. The night dream, as I mentioned earlier, is an example of such an existence or spatial realm *where we live.* From those experiences we can come to accept as genuine, *without prejudice,* all lived modes of human existence. We do not let our biases translate and explain one mode of being, for example, that manifested through imagination—to another mode—that manifested through linear logical thought.

What I am asking the reader to do is to take this intuitive and, at the same time, highly logical leap with me from the world of our linear thinking to the world of imagination. In this way we shall begin to construct a meaningful approach to knowledge as it applies to the mental suffering that is so characteristic of human experience. We shall move from a knowledge via the intellect to knowledge via lived experience; from understanding to wisdom, and in the end achieve a balance.

Notes

1. A form of waking dream to be described later.
2. I put the words *therapist* and *patient* in quotation marks because while the terms are convenient, I hope to show that these designations should

be changed in the therapeutic relationship. In order not to distract the reader I shall not use quotation marks for these terms as I proceed. It should be remembered, however, that I am using the two terms with qualifications.

3. Dr. David Shainberg alerted me to this distinction in a personal communication.

4. I am indebted to Cheryl Miller of Mt. Sinai Medical School, who, as my student, contributed this insight, which so helped me to clarify my own perspective on this subject.

5. The foregoing suggests that the designation of various cultures as "primitive" by western anthropologists has more to do with the prejudice of the designator in favor of linear logical (left brain) thinking than with intrinsic reasons. In these instances, those who operate differently from the designators are simply labelled "primitive."

6. I select the dream for expository purposes at this juncture, instead of imaginal experience, in that dreaming is an experience that most everyone shares. Of course I refer to the process and not to the content of dreaming.

7. The philosophies of empiricism and logical positivism both express the view that concrete reality is *the* reality instead of one reality among many.

Chapter 2

BACKGROUND

Prior to the advent of the Cartesian revolution in western thought, imagination was valued highly and its reality unquestioned. In fact, it was regarded as *the* major approach to the treatment of physical and emotional disorders (McMahon, 1976). Then Descartes came along and said, among other things, that imagination is "unreal" because it is not amenable to rational comprehension. The acceptance of Cartesian assumptions profoundly affected western medicine and psychotherapy, which since then has valued emperical experience above all. As yet there has been no systematic attempt to correct this imbalance. The very first requirement is that we attempt to correct the distorted semantic appreciation of the terms *imagination, imaginal, image,* and *imagery.*

As Corbin astutely pointed out (1972):

> Imaginary from Latin usage is equated with what is "unreal"... something outside of being and existing... Contrast this to the *Imaginal Realm* ... *A lived experience in space; a space that*

transcends concrete location and defies measureability [my emphasis]. This space provides the link for levels or planes of realities which also quite naturally remove us from the dimension of time that is measured by the movement of the clock ... A mode of existence whose act of being is an expression of its presence in these worlds. ... The image world is ontologically real and as real as the world of the senses. It uses its own faculty of perception namely imaginative power having a noetic value. Ontologically imagination is a function of the imaginal realm and is more immaterial than the sensible world. ... In the realm of analogical knowledge Imagination is the vehicle that allows penetration from outside to inside. (p. 1, 7)

Eastern Uses

In oriental life there is no question about the reality of imagery and imagination.[1] There has always been an acceptance of the value, power, and function of the image. One of the reasons for this acceptance derives from the general philosophy of life that informs oriental cultures. Briefly, one fundamental premise of oriental philosophy is expressed by the phrase "I am." By extension therefore, everything is. If everything is (that is, has an existence), then imagination has an existence. The major premise of post-Cartesian western philosophy is "I think, therefore I am," making the rational thought process the yardstick by which all thought is measured. Instead of being troubled by the imaginal, easterners accept its validity and are then free to explore its nature experientially. By doing so they can learn a lot about the human existence and establish ways of integrating imaginal life into the everyday practice of living. Some of these cultures, most notably the Chinese, Tibetan, and Islamic, have a great affinity for the imaginal.

The great Chinese book *I Ching* or *Book of Changes* has been *the* major influence on all Chinese life over the past 4,000 years.[2] It is constructed of eight fundamental images, related to elements of the natural world such as wind, water, mountain, flame, etc. This book comprises 64 hexagrams and commentaries.[3] The user throws 49 yarrow stalks while concentrating only on the question he wants answered. The resulting pattern of stalks indicates which hexagram to consult. The hexagrams are believed to contain all the knowledge of human existence and represent the nature of mankind in general as well as the individual thrower. The general is linked to the particular because the Chinese believe that (1) there is no distinction between inner and outer; (2) the throwing of the stalks, while aleatory, transcends the limitations of time and space so that man and nature are momentarily united.

Tibetan Buddhism also makes striking use of the imagination. In Tibetan practice,[4] one turns away for a time from the external world of concrete reality and attempts to turn one's senses inward, there to find other levels of consciousness, each populated by its particular inhabitants. There one encounters "other worldly creatures" of various kinds. There is a recognition (re-cognition, a knowing again of what was known before) of the essential unity of all existence and a corresponding diminution of the personal "I".

These imaginal recognitions are graphically and vividly portrayed in Tibetan art works called Tangka. There the entire panoply of psychological life is etched against the background of the sacred (symbolically displayed) with which it forms an indelible unity. Again, these realms of consciousness imaginally perceived and experienced are viewed as perfectly real and imbued not only with great meaning, but also with tremendous influence over the conduct of everyday life.[5]

Moving further west but still remaining in the orient, we come upon the imagination in the context of Judaism and its close neighbor Islam. The backbone of Jewish life is the Torah. The Torah embraces both the law and its historical and cultural tradition that governs the daily behavior of Jews as well as spiritual and esoteric knowledge about the nature of reality. This second form of knowledge is called Kabbalah. It is within this context that Rabbi Akiba in the first century, utilizing a form of spiritual work called "throne mysticism," traveled through mental spheres called "palaces" where visual imaginal experiences would ensue. Also, Abraham Aboulafia, in the thirteenth century, used imagination exercises to visualize letters of the Hebrew alphabet seeing them turned into various forms. But unlike other great cultures such as the Chinese, Japanese, Indian, and North American Indian, which have achieved an interdigitation of these two forms to enrich and enhance everyday life, Judaism for many reasons has always stressed the cultural and historical or legal and ethical aspects of its tradition at the expense of the imaginal.[6]

Western Uses

A little noticed trend in the treatment of emotional disturbance began to emerge in Europe in the 1930s. By that time, the teachings of Freud and other analysts had been so deeply assimilated in Europe and elsewhere that little attention was paid to the work of individual therapists in Germany and France who practiced independently and in isolation. They sought to incorporate into their treatment both the practical mental discipline of meditation as well as an understanding of the prevailing psychodynamics. The aim was to introduce notions of eastern psychology into a western cultural tradition. The important contributors have been Carl Happich (1965), Robert Desoille (1966), Wolfgang Kretschmer (1965), Hanscarl Leuner (1969, 1975), Roberto Assagioli (1965), and C. G. Jung (1954).

Carl Happich and Robert Desoille both evolved their techniques in the 1930s. Of the two, Desoille had been the more prolific writer but most of his writing is as yet untranslated from the original French. Desoille called his method *"Rêve Éveillé Dirigé"* or directed waking dream. He devised a set of motifs —mountain, cave, meadow, and so on—which he asked the patient to explore.

Desoille devised imaginal motifs to help the individual experience directly what he considered the fundamental aspects of existence. These are:

1. One's primary characteristics
   a. a man would look at a sword
   b. a woman would hold a vessel or container
2. One's more suppressed characteristics
   a. both sexes would descend into the ocean
3. Coming to terms with the parent of the opposite sex
   a. a man would descend into a cave to find a witch or sorceress
   b. a woman would descend into a cave to find a wizard or magician
4. Coming to terms with the parent of the same sex
   a. a man would descend into a cave to find a wizard or magician
   b. a woman would descend into a cave to find a witch or sorceress
5. Coming to terms with societal restraints
   a. both sexes would descend into a cave to find a dragon
6. Coming to terms with the oedipal situation
   a. a man would be Prince Charming in the castle of Sleeping Beauty
   b. a woman would be Sleeping Beauty

The method presented in this book deviates from Desoille's in one essential particular (among others): the experience to be used comes from the patient and specifically, from the patient's dream life. It is the patient, therefore, not the therapist, who supplies and determines the mode of expression to be used.

Both Happich and Desoille (as well as the others previously mentioned, except for Jung) used a meditational relaxation procedure at the beginning of each session so that the patient could probe mental imagery in a state of altered consciousness[7] considered to be different from the state we ordinarily experience in waking life. They reported that in this state, patients would have easier access to visual images that they felt often produced intense emotional responses. Their methods were substantially the following: the patient was to lie on a couch (preferably) or recline in a lounge chair, positioned so that he would not face the therapist. He then relaxed by using a simple meditation technique that consisted primarily of regulated breathing. The patient was then told to imagine a place such as a meadow, forest, mountain, or body of water. He was then to place himself in this locale and imagine performing some activity there. For example, at the meadow or forest, the patient would walk through and describe to the therapist what he saw, heard, touched, tasted, smelled, and felt. Or the patient would be asked to climb the mountain and describe the scene and whatever might be the accompanying emotional experience. At the body of water, the patient would be asked to dive in, pick up any object found lying on the bottom, and bring it up to the surface. The patient would take this object onto the shore, examine it, and report the findings to the therapist. The patient might be asked to walk through the forest or meadow, or to climb a hill or mountain with this object while continuing to describe his experience. These excursions were called directed waking dreams.[8] Hanscarl Leuner (1969, 1975), a German psychoanalyst, has combined this approach with analytic technique. He has reported numerous successful treatments completed within a period of six months; the patients have remained stable over a follow-up period of six years.

    Leuner attempts to enlarge Desoille's method by increasing the number of motifs originally described by Desoille. Leuner's technique, *guided affective imagery* (GAI), uses 10 motifs, one of which is suggested to the patient, who lies on a couch, at the beginning of a session:

1. Being in a meadow (a fresh start)
2. Climbing a mountain (mastery of the life situation)
3. Following a brook upstream to its source or down-

stream to the ocean (the flow of psychic energy and potential for psychic development)
4. A house (symbol of the person; a castle suggests grandiosity, a rude hut a lack of self-esteem)
5. A close relative (relationship to family)
6. For a male patient, a rosebush; for a female patient, an empty road in the country (sexual feelings)
7. A lion (aggression)
8. A person of the same sex (the ideal self)
9. A dark forest or the entrance of a cave (deeply repressed feelings; a witch or giant usually appears)
10. A swamp in a corner of the meadow (repressed instinctual, archaic feelings concerning sexual desires)

In his latest report published in English (1975), Leuner provides some data on the outcome of cases where patients were evaluated before and after the use of guided affective imagery. This group was compared to a control group being treated for the same manifest symptoms but without the use of GAI. He appears to demonstrate that the symptoms abate significantly faster with imagery work than with other techniques.

None of the authors discussed thus far mentions any use of dream analysis that departs from, or extends, Freud's formulations. Roberto Assagioli (1965), however, the founder of psychosynthesis, added a new device to obtain associations from dream elements. Basically, he would have the patient carry on a conversation with someone met in the dream, or have the patient undergo an extended imagery session beginning with an unresolved or conflictual incident from the dream. Assagioli's followers place less emphasis on dreams than psychoanalysts do. They use an imagery technique of putting oneself in another's place and carrying out the behavior in imagination (as opposed to Moreno, the founder of psychodrama, who had the patient act out his thoughts through role playing). Assagioli emphasized the conscious will, which could be strengthened by a series of mental exercises that can help the individual to overcome neurotic difficulties.

Jung also used a technique called *active imagination*, in which he would essentially ask the patient to complete a dream that was broken off or interrupted by the dreamer's waking up. At present there are a number of therapists in the United States and Europe, in addition to those just cited, who use some sort of imagery technique. Prominent in the United States is Jerome Singer.[9] Singer's method, which he uses with children as well as adults, takes daydreams as the jumping off point for exploring the patient's "inner life." He has not developed a technique of his own but combines behavior modification technique with some methods borrowed from various European practitioners whom he describes at length in his book. Perhaps Singer's singular contribution has been in the area of research where he has so ably demonstrated the physiological correlates of imagery experience (Singer and Pope, 1978).

Mardi Horowitz, a psychoanalyst working in the field of image formation, proposes an interesting thesis about human perception of the external world (1970). While a thesis as such can never be used as supporting evidence for the existence of a function like imagination within a phenomenological framework, nevertheless Horowitz's is of interest in orienting one's perspective toward waking dream. He suggests that all modes of perception be considered equally valid. No one mode is held to be superior to any other in terms of response to the percept, and conversely, no mode is held to be pathological. He posits three fundamental modes of response to the percept: lexical, visual, and actional. He goes on to say that the immediate percept of the human organism vis-à-vis the external world is received as a gestalt, i.e., as a total configuration. As this whole percept is mediated by the brain, the organism will respond according to one of the three fundamental modes. To "translate" via explanation from either the visual or actional mode to the lexical mode should be recognized as a bias of the psychological system that chooses to do so. While phenomenology does not accept the premise of stimulus-response psychology that underlies Horowitz's work, it does support his contention that perception is fundamentally gestaltic in nature, and that the tendency to translate one mode into the "language" of the other (and thereby give primacy to it) is essentially a bias. In waking dream, no tendency of this sort exists. Moreover, waking dream rejects the idea that the modes are mutually exclusive, but rather, seeks to harmonize and synthesize all three modes.

Brain Investigations

David Galin (1974) has described how each cerebral hemisphere functions independently (with some overlap) and is linked to the other by the corpus callosum. Galin and others have suggested that the right cerebral hemispheric functioning is concerned with visual events, imagination, and emotion (Bogen, 1969). That hemisphere, therefore, mediates analogical "thinking," and perceives the whole of experience or gestalt, rather than breaking down experience into sequential units and compartmentalized frames of reference—the sort of operation associated with or mediated by left brain functioning. Further, it is understood from the phenomenological perspective that the brain is the translator of whatever mode of existence the human being is living at that time. That is, one can dwell in the linear thought mode or the imaginal realm at any given instant, and the brain receives and mediates that event.

The implication of current brain investigations is that right brain functions have been suppressed in western culture where the left hemispheric activity prevails and has become the standard against which all other mental activity and human behavior is measured. The action of unifying the two halves, of harmonizing the two functions, is really the locus of our free will and thereby our freedom. If this be so, then the action of imaginal work as manifested most pronouncedly by waking

dream allows us a means by which we can escape those habitual tendencies that our social conditioning has inculcated in us.
Karl Pribram's (1971, 1979) findings substantiate this view. This noted neuropsychologist has elaborated what he calls the holographic model of neural behavior. He bases his work on the discovery of holography by Dennis Gabor in the 1940's (for which Gabor won the Nobel Prize), a method of lensless photography in which the light waves scattered by an object are recorded as an interference pattern on a photographic plate. When the plate, now a holographic field, is placed in a coherent light beam, i.e., a laser, the original object is regenerated and a three-dimensional image appears suspended in space. Without the use of this coherent sensory stimulus the plate looks like a meaningless pattern of swirls. Also, the photographic plate can be broken into many pieces and any one fragment will furnish the three dimensional image of the original object when the coherent stimulus is applied to it.[10] ("Coherent" means a sensory stimulus of one wave length only.) (Fig. 2.1).

Pribram (1979) suggests that "the physical universe and our brains have in common an order or reality that is similar in organization to holograms" (p. 83). In this model, "visual memory is composed of wave forms and organized like the hologram so that the memory becomes activated when the right set of wave forms is transmitted from the eye" (p. 79). In other words, the brain mathematically constructs concrete reality by interpreting frequencies *from another dimension,* a realm of meaningful, patterned, primary reality that transcends time and space. Pribram believes that this paradigm of neural behavior explains some of the classical puzzles of brain science and also offers a new way of understanding our perception of reality.

Pribram's model also contributes to understanding the action and efficacy of waking dream. Waking dream takes place in a level of reality different from that of the concrete world. This level is the correlate of Pribram's "other dimension." "Brain viewed as a hologram" is related to an underlying prin-

48   WAKING DREAM THERAPY

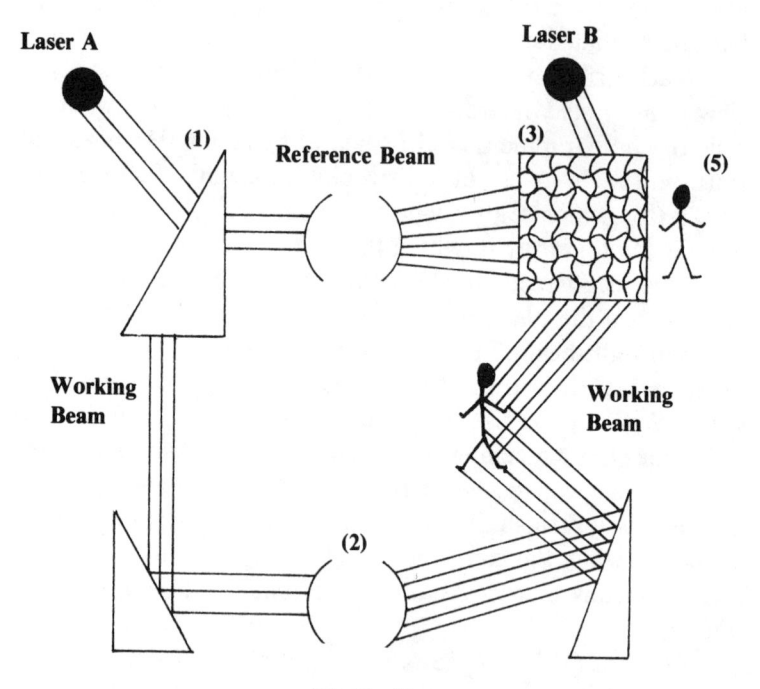

Working Beam

A laser beam (laser A), or any other coherent sensory source, is fired through a semi-mirror (1). The resulting beam is deflected in two directions. One beam, called the reference beam, registers directly on a photographic plate (3) after going through a lens (2) which merely serves to widen the beam. It registers on the photographic plate as a swirl of energy or interference pattern. The other beam, called the working beam, is deflected off additional semi-mirrors while going through a lens (2) merely serving to widen the beam. This beam hits an object in space—say a human being (4)—and the beam is then deflected to the photographic plate where it meets the reference beam and is registered also as a swirl of energy or interference pattern. If a laser (laser B) is fired at the photographic plate what will occur is that behind the plate will appear the image of the human being three dimensionally suspended in space. (5) If the plate were broken into fragments and a laser was fired at any one fragment the three-dimensional image would appear suspended in space. If the plate were further broken into fragments and a laser fired at any one fragment the three-dimensional image would appear suspended in space but less distinct. Thus, the part CONTAINS the whole. The universe is felt to be holographic by a number of physicists working in the area of subatomic and quantum physics who feel that this paradigm is more explanatory of events in microsomic reality.

Figure 2.1   Hologram (Lensless Photography)

ciple of waking dream and the imaginal realm in general, which is that the brain is the mediating organ for human experience. As defined here, "mind" is used in the sense that David Bohm expresses it when discussing the "enfolded order" of reality (see below). Brain occurs within mind, and mediates the movement of mind.

Imagination acts as a laser beam that activates and clarifies the reality that exists beyond our physicality. This reality ordinarily appears to be an incoherent swirl or interference pattern of which we tend to be unaware. This interference pattern, however, contains all the available information about the universe in which we live. Like the hologram, it discloses its information only when the laser beam, i.e., imagination, Corbin's "organ of perception lying behind concrete reality," strikes it directly.

The interference pattern yields up a three-dimensional form. Our senses then apprehend this form and relay the information to the brain. What has been apperceived is capable of translation into action in the world and can be available to us as retrieved data. This information gives direction to what one needs to do for self-development and fulfillment in life.

In my view, however, there is a schism in how the right and left hemispheres mediate the information afforded by the universe. The right brain apprehends holistically while the left interprets. Gazzaniga has devised an experiment to show this difference: the right and left hemispheres are independently shown the same picture, a man holding a gun to the head of another man. When the right brain alone sees the picture,[11] the subject describes the two men and the gun as "a holdup." When the left brain alone sees the picture, the subject interprets, infers, and interpolates an explanation, such as a bank hold up with assistant robbers pointing machine guns at the tellers while herding them into another room, and so on.

At the point of translation, linear thought can tell us *how* to use what we know. Deterministic logic, i.e., material-efficient causality, can direct the execution of our actions in the concrete world. *This is the appropriate use of linear thought.* It is inappropriate to use linear thought to explain or interpret, or "analyze" an event.

David Bohm (1980), the nuclear physicist, has developed a concept of "enfolded" and "unfolded" orders of reality, one that enriches both the phenomenon of waking dream, and its underlying holographic principle. He views "unfolded" order as a secondary manifestation of reality but *not its source*. These *appearances* of reality are abstracted from an *intangible*, not readily seen, flux, constituted not of parts but rather of an inseparable interconnectedness, synthesis, or "enfolded" reality. Bohm adds that any science that attempts to discover primary physical laws by breaking the world into its parts cannot succeed.

The aim of waking dream is to move from unfolded, physical reality—without denying its authenticity—toward the enfolded order, the source of reality. Consonant with Bohm's ideas, waking dream aims at synthesis, not analysis. One of its effects is to bring about a balancing of hemispheric functioning by accenting the activity of the so-called minor hemisphere.

THE BRIDGE

A plenitude of psychological techniques have been advanced that purport to promote healing. However, none of the currently evolved systems in vogue have been able to demonstrate that they are able to sustain such an outcome over an appreciable period of time. A primary reason for this may be found in the root of the word "heal," which is the same as that of "holy," 'health," and "whole." So, in order to be whole, a man should be restored to health by a process that includes the holy. This idea has been totally neglected, if not repudiated, by most western therapeutic systems. Freudian analysis, for example, the prototype for most of the western forms of psychotherapy,[12] is generaly arrayed against the experience of the holy or sacred, both in theory and in practice. Freud personally felt that religion was inimical to the interests of science, of which he considered psychoanalysis to be part. Today most psychologies reduce religious experience to "an infantile longing for merging with an omnipotent and all protecting parent." It is clear that, at least publicly, organized psychiatry and psychology view religious belief and practice as "neurotic."

That being the case, one hardly expects the religious and spiritual potentials to be incorporated into the psychoanalytic system. Furthermore, Freud believed that all knowledge is accessible through logic and reasoning with words (i.e., content of linear thought). It is well known that many religious and spiritual experiences which convey knowledge to the individual (such as Moses' at Mt. Sinai) are not describable in words and frequently are attainable *only* when the content of linear thought is slowed, stopped, emptied, that is, when one is able to stop giving name and form to what one perceives; for naming and forming are the fundamental characteristics of linear thought.

It is when such nonlinear thinking is embraced that a holistic experience can happen. It is here then that a possibility of healing asserts itself through an experience which abrogates the activity of linear thought. If this is so, and waking dream supports this contention, then psychoanalysis can offer only partial healing and at worst, perpetuates the fragmentation and suffering the patient initially brings to therapy because it does not offer the possibility for nonlinear activity to balance the linear emphasis of analysis.

If therapy tries to invalidate man's relationship to God, it does so at the expense of dissipating our fundamental wholeness. If this is the case then the whole picture of a man's potentials cannot be addressed, leaving therapy incomplete. Let me give a homely comparison. A manager in a factory is expected to master three major relationships to be successful. He must understand the community, i.e., the product and the consumer and the relationship of the factory to its environment. He must know his employees, i.e., understand those who work for him and his responsibility towards them. He must also understand his relationship to his superiors. Only then can he satisfactorily accomplish his task. For a man to "know himself," an avowed aim of therapy, he must get to know himself in relation to his world at large, those whose care is entrusted to him, and those (or the one) to whom his care is entrusted. This latter can be called his Maker.[13] In order to live successfully, *all three* relationships must be taken into account.

Any therapy that fails to deal with all three cannot effectively promote healing, health, and wholeness. To repudiate the idea of a Maker locates man as personal "I" at the center of experience beholden to no one and denies allegiance to anything outside that personal "I." In such a case, how can any therapy (or psychological system) ever hope to come to grips with the problem of "narcissism," a term that has come to be the central descriptive element in the problems of the so-called borderline disturbance, schizoid disturbance, many character disturbances including narcissistic character, psychotic depressive disturbance, and perhaps most importantly, schizophrenic disturbances. By sustaining the supreme importance of the personal "I," narcissism is encouraged rather than overcome.

To approach the problem of the personal "I," of which narcissism is one manifestation, one requires a different perception. Martin Heidegger took a psychophilosophical step toward this different perception when he pointed out the importance of the not-"I" field which, when understood and grasped, helps to diminish the significance of the personal "I" (1971):

> ... Spaces, and with them space as such—"space"—are always provided for already within the stay of mortals. Spaces open up by the fact that they are let into the dwelling of man. To say that mortals *are* is to say that *in dwelling* they persist through spaces by virtue of their stay among things and locations. And only because mortals pervade, persist through, spaces by their very nature are they able to go through spaces. But in going through spaces we do not give up our standing in them. Rather, we always go through space in such a way that we already experience them by staying constantly with near and remote locations

and things. When I go toward the door of the lecture hall I am already there, and I could not go to it at all if I were not such that I am there. *I am never here only, as this encapsulated body; rather, I am there, that is, I already pervade the room* [my emphasis], and only thus can I go through it. Even when mortals turn "inward," taking stock of themselves, they do not leave behind their belonging to the fourfold (earth, sky, divinities, mortals). When, as we say, we come to our senses and reflect on ourselves, we come back to ourselves from things *without ever abandoning* our stay among things. Indeed, the loss of rapport with things that occurs in states of depression would be wholly impossible if ever such a state were not still what it is as a human state: that is, a staying *with* things. Only if this stay already characterizes human being can the things among which we are also *fail* to speak to us, *fail* to concern us any longer [author's emphasis] (p. 157).

Another question that needs to be addressed by therapy in connection with the religious and spiritual possibility of man's existence is that of "conscious" versus "unconscious" activity. These terms have defied consistent definition and have been used in varying unsatisfactory contexts in human psychology. Since "consciousness" is so difficult to grasp psychologically, a serious question arises about its value. One major question is whether the field of inquiry called psychology can reliably investigate an element it finds so fundamental to its own existence. Is an unprejudiced examination of one's own presuppositions possible?[14]

Another difficulty arises when "consciousness" is defined as an act of mind such as perception, memory, learning, etc. This assumes a definition of "mind" and an understanding of "consciousness" as a manifestation of "cognitive" action; "cognitive" action is further assumed to be a function of brain and to constitute mind. But do "consciousness" and "mind" reside in the brain? Do brain and mind function independently or does one serve the other? What of the eastern understanding of "consciousness" which sees it within a larger framework of "awareness"?

The definition of "consciousness" is irrelevant to imaginal

experience because it is assumed that imagination is real and that the individual lives, experiences, and recognizes this realm. "Consciousness" is accepted as a process that allows us to exist in concrete reality, but it is not used in this context as a psychological construct, nor is it needed as such. "Reality" itself is not a purely psychological term and does not elude definition in the context of waking dream. Here, "reality" is understood experientially rather than inferentially or logically. The experiential perspective acknowledges "reality" as absolute, objective, and subjective. Thus we avoid the usual bias of psychology that evaluates everything by the standard of what is measureable by the five senses in the concrete world. Instead of accepting only one reality, we become alert to *levels and varieties of reality.* If we accept the supposition of differing levels of reality (of course it is only a supposition until we experience the fact), we discover implications for psychotherapy.

One possibility is for a new perception of schizophrenic hallucinations. If we recognize this phenomenon as subjectively real for the patient, albeit not consensually shared, then we can ask the patient to describe his experience and share it in a nonjudgmental way. This sharing can help the therapist overcome his impulse to label ("crazy," "unrealistic," "psychotic," etc.) and establish instead an environment of some trust and mutuality. The distance between the two participants may be decreased in this way and the detachment of the therapist from his object of study, the patient, may be reduced.

Another, more general implication is that we can stop labelling and classifying. The taxonomy of pathology, arbitrary at best, automatically elevates the classifiers above the patients. If we admit the authenticity of all experience, we can stop this judgmental thinking and its attendant closure of open acceptance. When such closure becomes institutionalized, the field of psychotherapy can easily stagnate and wither.

Generally, "objective" or concrete reality[15] refers to those phenomena which can be consensually validated. For example, almost everyone would agree that the Empire State Building is on Fifth Avenue at 34th Street in New York City. Subjective reality is often nonconsensual and is not amenable to measurement.

I prefer to designate other realms of existence "levels of reality" rather than "levels of consciousness." Further, I use the term *existence* rather than *function* when discussing what happens on these levels or realms. These words focus on an essential principle of phenomenological work in general and waking dream work in particular: the individual *exists as the same person* in *different* levels of reality or realms of existence. This shift in attitude leads to an acceptance of intangible as well as tangible experience, which in turn can encourage a new understanding of subjective phenomena such as dreams. Such a shift in relating to our dream life, for example, may help to enrich our understanding of this important experience.[16]

The phrase "functions of consciousness" implies a personal "I" who is centrally important to the experience. This results from the ingrained tendency to regard all states of consciousness as a *departure* from this present state of waking consciousness, against which all other states are measured. Thus it is presupposed that the function of waking consciousness is *the* standard of reality, and that the function is owned by the individual as an object or thing. It has been suggested that the "I" who exists in different levels of reality is the personal "I." This is in part true, but *at the same time that the personal "I" exists it is being transcended by the experience of being in different realms, and by the realization that the personal "I" is an experience related specifically to one's existence as a physical being in the realm of concrete reality.* The terminology of this book reflects the assumption that all realms of experience are equally valid. We can explore these realms just as we do the physical, concrete world. We do so via imaginal exploration. Consciousness, then, is merely the process by which we move from one level of reality to another.

What then of the individual who becomes a patient exploring the imaginal realm? Current tradition equates physical man with the personal "I." By accepting different levels of reality and understanding that exploration of a *nonphysical sort*[17] takes place in those levels, one begins to appreciate *what can be experienced outside the limitations of the physical body.* It is then through experience that one comes to recognize that one is more than one's physicality. Note that I am not denying the importance of the physical body and our physical existence here on earth. Nothing could be further from the truth, for as we shall see, as the process of waking dream unfolds, the earth and our rootedness to it as human beings, existing here as physical forms, remains fundamentally important.

The realization of nonphysical processes in a nonphysical environment allows us to recognize that we exist *in* and *as* a particular mode of relatedness to whatever we encounter. The human "being"[18] can be said to be a vehicle for the manifestation of the imaginal level of reality.

One important by-product of this recognition is the opportunity to look at the critical problem of "narcissism" from a new perspective. If man is the vehicle for a flow of energy, or for the manifestation of a realm of reality, and one *experiences* this to be true, then one has escaped from the identification of the "I" with the physical objects of its perception, of which "narcissism" is one tendency.

As I see it, by trying to define and explain "narcissism," as Otto Kernberg (1975) and Heinz Kohut (1971, 1977), among others, have done, one falls into the trap of mistaking the abstraction for the concrete reality and concrete reality for the abstraction. "Narcissism" is merely a particular abstraction of the more general concrete reality which is the movement of linear thought with its tendency to *produce* images (to be enlarged on below) or the tendency of the personal "I" to identify itself with the object of its perception. But what is known must have a knower.[19] And the knower and the known (the subject and the object) can never be identical. What is known to the knower, therefore, including the physical body, can never *be* the knower. The I (knower-subject) who knows the object of perception—and the physical body is one of the most commonly known objects—cannot be what is known (object). But people tend to identify the personal "I" (knower) with what is perceived (object of perception). This always results in the personal "I" being thrust into the center of experience, thereby becoming "narcissistic." (In some people, this tendency is exaggerated and the personal "I," also called "ego," identifies more widely and becomes consequently more fragmented. The most extreme exaggeration of this process is schizophrenia, but this is by no means the only reason for schizophrenia.)

When Kernberg talks about "object" and "self" representations, he does so in the context of an "I" who *possesses* these things (object and self representations). According to Kernberg, the "I" (ego) *automatically identifies* with what it owns and may seek to get rid of its possessions if they are considered alien. The perceiver, from the outset, and unquestioningly, is identified with the object of his perception, and thus the movement toward "narcissism" is perpetuated. Kernberg's interpretation, or theory, unwittingly fosters the very movement he is trying to halt, because he has confused abstract and concrete realities.

To sort out this confusion, let us consider the movement of a steady stream. Within that movement, a turbulence results in the formation of rivulets or ripples. One might say that the rivulet or ripple is the concrete essential reality because it manifests and shows forth in an assertive way that captures our attention. The truth is that what appears in this forceful way, however, cannot be removed from the stream. And, in fact, when this exaggerated movement subsides, the stream still remains. That which appeared to have name and form actually changed and disappeared while what appeared formless continued on unchanged. What is formless and continues unchanged can be said to be the general, concrete, essential reality. What appeared to have form (i.e., real in an "objective" sense, having been given a name) was momentary and passing, but it is usually misperceived as the concrete essential reality. The rivulet was abstracted (removed out of) the stream and became the particulate form of the general, subject to change, decay, and impermanence. The fundamental principles of waking dream support this point of view: these principles hold that man (the particulate) is a vehicle for the imaginal realm (the general) and as such can also be the vehicle for manifesting that realm within the level of physical, concrete reality. Each man is important for the concrete functions he performs and in his attempts to enlighten himself. He often becomes confused by mistaking his particular contribution to the whole as the whole itself, however. He considers himself to be globally self-important (or grandiose) and fails to experience the humbling and sobering experience of his bubblelike existence, subject to decay and impermanence in the sea of endless change and flux.

Notes

1. It is important to recognize the essential distinction between "imagination" and "fantasy." This distinction will be spelled out more fully later when describing waking dream proper.

2. Ken Phillips, personal communication. Mr. Phillips is a physicist in charge of telecommunications worldwide for CitiCorp and is a teacher of the *I Ching*.

3. The hexagram is a six-line vertical abstract form constructed by solid (——) and parted (— —) lines, which represent male (——) and female (— —) principles or energies. These two lines form a trigram (the number three being used by the Chinese to represent synthesis), e.g.: ≡≡. This form is determined by throwing yarrow stalks and then using a simple mathematical computation which designates whether the line is male (Yang) or female (Yin). A second trigram is then determined and positioned above the first one. The upper line of a trigram represents heaven while the lower represents earth. Man (the thrower) is the agent through which the forces of heaven and earth intermingle. Thus, ≡≡≡ is an example of a hexagram. There are 64 such combinations. Each trigram represents an image as well, e.g., ≡≡ is heaven; ≡ ≡ is earth.

4. "Practice" in Tibetan life is not separate from psychology. However, their "psychology" focuses on the states of consciousness entered into via meditative practice rather than on the contents of consciousness, more specifically, waking consciousness, which is more the province of study of western psychology in general. "Consciousness" is a Buddhist term which I do not use for discussing imaginal phenomenology. I retain the term here for expository purposes regarding other phenomenological practices where it is an integral part of that vocabulary. Later on I shed the term in relation to waking dream in favor of "levels of reality." I would say that the "levels of reality" are apprehended through the process of altering the state of consciousness.

5. The reader who wants to explore this further might begin with *Foundations of Tibetan Mysticism* by Lama Govinda (New York: Samuel Weiser, 1974).

6. For the fullest, most comprehensive, and clearest description of kabbalistic practices see *Kabbalah: The Way of the Jewish Mystic* by Perle Epstein (New York: Doubleday, 1978). Gershon Scholem's *Major Trends in Jewish Mysticism* (New York: Schocken Books, 1941, 1961), the classic textbook of Jewish mysticism, contains several penetrating insights into the split between Kabbalah and mainstream Jewish life.

7. I use the term *consciousness* as a convenience for this present discussion. There is merit to questioning the validity of the term *altered consciousness* or *altered state of consciousness*. Such usage implies that the ordinary waking state itself is not an altered state and is, therefore, qualified to serve as the yardstick against which all other states should be measured. Such discussion will be reserved for another occasion.

8. There have been some attempts at theorizing about the action of these techniques from the psychiatric perspective, and I refer the reader to an article by P. Kosbab, Imagery techniques in psychiatry. *Arch. of Gen. Psych.*, 1974, 31, 282–290.

9. See J. Singer, *Imagery Techniques in Psychotherapy and Behavior Modification* (New York: Academic Press, 1974). This is the best available book in English on the various practitioners of imagery techniques. Another book of interest is that of P. Sheehan (ed.), *The Function and Nature of Imagery* (New York: Academic Press, 1972), which discusses experimental work done with regard to imagery. It should also be noted that at present there exists a *Journal of Mental Imagery* and an international society of practitioners in a field of therapeutics devoted exclusively to the practice of one imagery technique or another.

10. For a clear and concise explanation of the holographic principle, see *Stalking the Wild Pendulum* by Itzhak Bentov (New York: E. P. Dutton, 1977) and the journal *Re-Vision,* Vol. 1, #3–4, summer-fall 1978.

11. He has devised a special pair of glasses that allows alternately only the left (to right hemisphere) or right (to left hemisphere) visual field to be viewed by both eyes simultaneously.

12. Jung was not guilty of this failing. He paid a great deal of attention (too much, in fact) to the spiritual and religious side of man. His weakness was the complement of Freud's: he tended to ignore man's animalistic side and its role in behavior. He responded to this by noting that his therapy was really best suited for people over 40, when one has entered a phase of life where the intensity of sexual matters is more or less behind one and where religious and spiritual matters often take on more significance.

13. The importance will become even clearer when I come to the section on symbolism and its significance for waking dream.

14. Heisenberg's construct of uncertainty is related to this question: he said that the act of observation changes what is observed. Heisenberg's statement concerns the relationship of observer to observed in the world of "concrete reality," but it impinges on a serious problem in the subjective realm as well: the observer attempts to observe something he has already named; this naming presupposes certain assumptions that color his observation. And in the case of psychology, the observer has a stake in preserving that which stands as a pillar of his work.

15. The terms *concrete* and *objective* reality are interchangeable. I personally prefer concrete because it is more directly sensory whereas objective implies in fact a subjective attitude towards reality.

16. A saying in the Talmud has it that an unexamined dream is like an unopened letter.

17. Physical here means the *actual* movement of the concrete organism. Waking dream work uses the five senses as a function of imaginal work, as shall be explained more fully later on. Waking dream activity affects physiology, so that walking in an imaginal setting, for example, will be reflected in changes of musculature as measured by electromyography (Singer, 1978).

18. I use "being" here to mean physical existence. Human existence is defined direclty by its physical manifestation in a body that is intuitively recognized as human and cannot possibly be misperceived as anything else.

19. Some posit an "unconscious" that is by definition unknown and therefore not an object of perception. But to postulate an unconscious, you must know that one exists. If it is known to exist, then it is an object of perception, and by definition it is known from the outset and therefore can never be not known. The shift in this regard must come from taking this notion of unconscious out of its logical framework and putting it into an experiential one where we can speak of "unconsciousness" as a process. There are many dilemmas for me within this whole issue, chief among which is that of getting bogged down in a psychological term that leads automatically to endless argumentation; "unconscious" has become a convenient vehicle to explain any event of human existence that deterministic cause and effect thinking cannot account for.

Chapter 3

JOURNEYING

Waking dream and guided exercise are journeys to a different realm of existence. Waking dream, the primary focus of this book, comes directly out of the participant's night dreams: the dreamer is asked to choose the element of his dream that he finds most significant, compelling, or striking, and this element becomes the image that begins waking dream exploration. Guided exercise, in contrast, begins with a motif suggested by the instructor. Both are conducted in the same way toward the same goals. Both produce visible behavioral change in everyday life after a brief course of treatment.

As waking dream therapy progresses, the night dreams become more like waking dreams. The dreamer becomes more aware of himself as a participant, he is less passive than in ordinary night dreams, and he asserts his will more. This growing similarity between night dreams and waking dreams is significant because it points to an openness of flow between night dreams, imagination, and waking life, and it indicates a transformation in the perception of reality. The continuity between the three states is a sign that waking dream work is taking effect.

In contrast to meditation, which relies on the loss of ordinary sensory awareness in order to apprehend or experience other levels of reality, waking dream relies on the use of our five senses, which bring us in contact with the world of concrete reality. We recognize from experience that we go where our senses go: they lead us, fill us with desire, and prompt us to relate to whatever we encounter. In waking dream work, our senses move away from the world of concrete reality. As the senses discover other realities, we can begin to explore these worlds in the same way we explore the concrete world. By using the senses, we stay grounded within a known biological framework.

At the beginning of waking dream therapy, I ask the person to formulate what he wishes to get from the work, or what questions he wants answered. Waking dream thus provides a focus or intention about what will be achieved. This focusing is also a form of self-induction toward personal development. Many people find it difficult to specify what they want, and their difficulty indicates a diffuseness in their lives. Some preparatory dialogue may be required to help them define their goals.

I generally ask the patient to list one or three things. Two is avoided because it suggests inwardly a splitting or a duality. One conveys the sense of unity, and three that of synthesis. Sometimes a person will list more than three items, but usually they can be regrouped into three major interests.

When the goals are achieved or the questions answered to the satisfaction of the patient, the therapy is finished. If the person returns in the future, he always comes to learn something new. The new quest may be a transformation of the previous achievement, but it always takes place on a more profound level of personal development.

Both waking dream and guided exercise are conveniently divided, for didactic and practical purposes, into three stages.

Stage 1: Induction

Induction is generally a charged term in our culture and in the scientific community particularly. It is often associated with hypnosis and thereby with the loss of will. However, waking dream is very different from hypnosis;[1] it is a state of active will and alertness in another realm of existence, a most unusual combination. Induction in waking dream helps the participant turn his attention and sensory awareness away from the world of habitual reality toward a different reality. A light relaxation state occurs that reinforces the turning-within movement required for this kind of dream exploration. As in traditional therapy, external stimuli should be blotted out as much as possible. The aim here is toward a state of inner-directed attention that quiets the participant and breaks the rhythm of his habitual activity.

However this relaxation state differs physiologically from those of hypnosis or sleep. Benson and Wallace (1972); Corby, Roth, Zarcone, Kopell (1978); Hirai (1974), among many others, have all studied these differences. Benson and Wallace studied transcendental meditation practitioners and found a marked reduction of blood, pulse rate, and oxygen consumption; carbon dioxide elimination was decreased, blood lactate levels declined precipitously, and galvanic skin resistance increased markedly. The general picture is a highly relaxed, wakeful condition with some reduction of heart rate. EEG tracings showed a marked intensification of alpha waves and in some subjects there was also an increase in theta wave activity.

Simply put, the varying waves seen on electroencephalographic recordings are of four types: alpha, beta, delta, and theta. These waves are not state-dependent, that is, they occur regardless of the state of consciousness of the individual. Theta waves are those seen in imaginal experiences, while alpha are found in meditative experiences, beta in anxiety and agitation, and delta in conditions of physical illness.

In contrast, hypnotic states show no noticeable change in

the metabolic index, while in sleep, oxygen consumption decreases only after several hours and carbon dioxide in the blood increases significantly. The EEG of the hypnotized person shows random alpha waves with more prominent beta type activity (Hirai, 1974).[2]

Corby and his associates studied a group practicing Tantric Yoga meditation. In common with Benson and Wallace, they discovered increased skin resistance, a lowering of oxygen consumption, and an increase in alpha and theta waves. In contrast, however, they found an increase in heart rate, a higher amplitude of respiratory rate, no EEG-defined sleep, and autonomic activation, whereas Benson and Wallace found autonomic relaxation. Corby's group concluded that the physiological effects of meditation depend on the proficiency of the meditator: while inexperienced meditators tend to relax, proficient meditators show a lessened response to external stimuli but also an arousal of autonomic activation. In other words, meditative techniques seem to give access to a variety of physiological and subjective states depending on the technique and proficiency of the meditator.

To achieve light relaxation in waking dream, the person sits with his back straight in a sturdy, straight-backed chair, places his feet flat on the floor, and settles his arms well back on the arms of the chair. This is because erect posture of the back and body facilitates breathing, the ultimate vehicle for induction. He then closes his eyes to keep out distracting visual perceptions[3] and begins to breathe evenly and regularly through the nose. As he does this, he is told to imagine that as he breathes out he is breathing out waste products from inside of his body. The waste products emerge as carbon dioxide, which he is to see as *grey smoke,* like cigarette smoke, drifting away in the air. As he breathes in, he is to take in the pure oxygen that nourishes and purifies the body in the form of a *blue-golden* light formed by a mixture of bright golden sun and cloudless blue sky. Exhalation is through the mouth.

As he does this, he is told that he begins to form a cycle

of rhythmical breathing, taking in the blue-golden light and breathing out the grey smoke; this allows him to feel relaxed, calm, tranquil, and peaceful. He is further told that as he breathes in this even, regular way, he is breathing in all that is pure and breathing out all that is impure; he is breathing in all that is healthy and breathing out all that is unhealthy; breathing in all that is nourishing and breathing out all that is waste.

He is told:

> As you form this even and regular cycle of breathing, *know*[4] that you are collecting your thoughts and mind and are turning your attention inward away from the external world.... as you do so, you turn your senses and attention inward, you imagine that you are leaving the external world and moving toward the center of your being. You are moving toward the center of your awareness, to the core of your existence, and as you do so, you focus on your breathing, taking in the blue-golden light and breathing out the grey smoke; taking in what's good and breathing out what's not good for you. And as you breathe in this even and regular way, you will find yourself moving more and more into the center of your existence, to the core of your being. And as you do so you find your senses and your attention moving further and further inward. As you breathe, you find yourself developing an even and regular cycle of breathing.
>
> You find yourself breathing as one with all creatures in the universe. And as you breathe you find yourself breathing as one with all who were, who are, and who will ever be in all it is you want to do or become. And as you breathe in this even and regular way and turn your attention inward, you find yourself feeling relaxed, calm, peaceful, and tranquil.
>
> There's a sense of centeredness and balance that begins to develop in you as you find yourself feeling completely relaxed and calm and a sense of well-being begins to grow in you and a feeling of harmony begins to descend over you as you find yourself turning more and more toward the center of your existence, toward the core of your awareness, to that place where it is peaceful and quiet and still, and where there is no thought and everything is calm and tranquil and peaceful. And as you breathe in this even and regular way, you find yourself moving more and more toward the center of your being, to the core of your awareness.

And as you do so, you imagine the blue light that you've been breathing in travelling to all parts of your body via your bloodstream, enriching all of the cells in your body, and forming halos of blue light around all the red blood cells. The blue light is travelling throughout the bloodstream to all the parts of your being, nourishing, purifying, and cleansing you physically, emotionally, and spiritually. You imagine the blue light coming out of your heart into the great vessels of your body; travelling throughout the great vessels of your body to all the smaller vessels. So that the blue light travels to all parts of your being, nourishing and purifying you and making your whole body feel completely relaxed.

And as you see this blue light travel to all parts of your body, you find your toes relaxing, you find your feet relaxing, you find your ankles relaxing; your calves and your legs and your knees and your thighs, your groin, your abdomen are all relaxed. You find your chest relaxed and your shoulders and your neck, your upper back, lower back, buttocks, upper arms, elbows, forearms, wrists, hands, fingers, head and face, all completely relaxed as the blue light reaches all parts of your body via the bloodstream, nourishing and purifying you and making you feel completely relaxed and calm.

And a sense of energy and strength and radiance begins to fill you and a feeling of power and stillness and quietness and calm pervades all through your being. And as you fill with this blue light, imagine it extending past your fingertips creating an aura of sapphire blue light around your entire body, filling you up outside of your body as it has inside with this nourishing and purifying blue light. It fills you up outside your body with energy, power, radiance, and strength, so that you fill both inside and outside with blue light. And as you fill with this blue light outside and inside your body, you immediately become aware that your body is a vehicle for blue light that allows the linking of inside blue light with the outside blue light and that your body is a bridge for this blue light and a vehicle for the light. So that you are becoming as blue light. You become as blue light full of energy, power, radiance, and strength.

Imagine yourself now leaving this chair and leaving this room, and find yourself going back into your dream, and find yourself at this place where you've arrived (give specifics of the predetermined setting and where you have stopped). And describe to me what you see, what you hear, what you feel, and any other sensory experience that may occur. And please don't move your hands.[5]

This marks the end of the induction. The therapist emphasizes relaxation (calmness, tranquillity), silence (stillness, quietness), and oneness (harmony, unity, synthesis). The induction period takes about two to three minutes at the beginning of the course of treatment, and no more than one minute after the subject is familiar with the process.

STAGE 2: GOING AND RETURNING

The first part is the actual journey of waking dream, called the *going*. This experience lasts about 30 to 40 minutes, and it is customary to tell the individual at the outset just how long the journey will be. This information greatly helps the traveller to achieve what he has set out to do. It provides an *intention* that propels him to make the discoveries that are important for him. The average person can endure the great expenditure of energy entailed in this kind of work for 30 to 40 minutes, although some people tire earlier than this, and some just get going at this point.

The major exception is the first waking dream experience, where the journey should last for one and one-half to two hours. The central reason is that the patient is not accustomed to this kind of work and is often skeptical. The activity of imagination is a dormant function for most of us in this culture. It is a practice like any other and effort is required to feel comfortable in this realm. The long first journey helps reorient habitual thinking. This length also helps the subject move away from the more familiar realm of fantasy, where one has a tendency to languish.

The second part of the journey consists of the *returning* to the here and now of the waking world. Generally, the subject will give some sort of indication that he is ready to return. He may say that he feels tired, a definite sign that he should cease and return. He may say explicitly that he does not wish to go on. Or, he may have accomplished what he set out to do for that particular time and does not need, for the moment, to go farther. The instructor has to pay attention to the facial expression of the explorer during the imaginal experience. If he notes the muscles around the jaw slackening or the muscles around the eyes twitching, these are indications that the explorer is physiologically weakening, and they signal that the journey cease and the return commence.

The travel back, the *returning,* should be brisk. The subject should return as though he is flying or hovering over the setting he has just traversed without describing it. He returns along the same route even if it was originally scary, anxiety-provoking, or ugly. The explorer is told that he can see what disturbed him in a new way because he is returning with new perception and understanding. Returning by the same route helps refresh and increase the memory. Returning means bringing the senses back to everyday life.

The physiological changes produced in the going reverse themselves in the returning. Body temperature often drops in waking dream and must be brought back to normal. If the voyager feels exhausted at the end of the work, he is encouraged to drink some caloric beverage for quick energy and reentry into the physical world. If he feels dizzy, he may be asked to lie down. If he feels tense, he may require more eduction work (see below). Other complaints, e.g., headache, nausea or other abdominal distress, or great hunger, may arise, but these are minor and temporary. They all relate to the great effort expended in this work.

When the subject comes to his point of departure, he is asked to comment on anything he may have noted or experienced in returning. He is then asked to return to the chair in which he sits and to open his eyes and *see* on whatever blank surface is opposite him, the apex, or climax, or high point of the event of which he was just a part. He is asked to see himself in that same situation and to reexperience it *without speaking*. Often, he will see or recognize something that he can articulate to the instructor when he re-enters the waking world in a fully alert state after the eduction is completed.

STAGE 3: EDUCTION

After the subject opens his eyes and looks for about 15 to 30 seconds, the eduction begins. He is told:

> As the image begins to fade, you find yourself breathing evenly and regularly. As you do so you find your feet feeling heavy and pressing into the carpet, your arms feeling heavy and pressing into the arms of the chair. Your whole body is relaxing as all of the tension goes out of your muscles and you find your body sinking into the chair. Your shoulders feel heavy, as though a weight were pushing them down. You find yourself coming back to the here and now feeling awake, attuned, alert, and aware to all that is going on around you in this environment. You come back to the here and now feeling refreshed, renewed, rejuvenated, and reborn like a new person in mind, body, and spirit. You come back feeling calm, peaceful, tranquil, and relaxed, full of vim, vigor, and vitality. You feel energy and no tension. There is a sense of unity within and without, and a feeling of centeredness, and harmony is present. As you experience this sense of well-being and contentment you feel all of the tension going out of your body as your muscles feel completely relaxed and loose.

As eduction proceeds, the subject will emit little tell-tale signs that he is back in his usual waking state. The eyelids will flutter or he will exercise his fingers or roll his head or stretch his arms. At this point the instructor asks if there is anything he wants to say, comment on, or ask. If not, and this commonly happens, the session proper is concluded. Eduction should take as long as induction (see p. 68).

The patient is then asked to write and draw the event in a standard, unlined school notebook. The first page is inscribed with what the person wants to get, know, understand, achieve, or learn from his work. The patient then draws a vertical line down the center of the rest of the pages, front and back. He dates and titles the report at the top, e.g., Waking Dream #2, Mar. 14, 1981, and describes everything he remembers on the left side of the page, front and back. With colored pens (or crayons, pencils), he then draws the significant images that correspond to his text on the right-hand side of the page. He should label his drawings if they need clarification. If he has any spontaneous thoughts or feelings while drawing, he should include these in the right-hand column. He signs his name at the bottom. This work stamps the experience as his; it is something that belongs to him (Fig 3.1).

Night dreams should also be recorded in the same notebook in the same way. This is difficult and many do not even attempt it. Some write out the dreams but very few write and draw them. Sometimes patients who do not draw dreams at first begin to do so as waking dream therapy proceeds. Patients may wake up in the night in order to record their dreams but this is not at all necessary and is detrimental to physical well-being.

Frequently the person wants to put off reproducing the exercise. Often this is because he wants to savor the experience and fears that by recording it, the experience will be dissipated or lost to him. But the energy, if not put out in the world, is then lost for constructive action and returns to the general field of energy that informs our existence. Sometimes the person has a habit of not sharing or a habit of not finishing anything because of a deficiency of will.

I ask the patient for a photocopy (in color) of the work so that I can go over it on my own and keep a record from which progress can be gauged. I ask the patient to look over his work at home as a preparation for our subsequent meeting(s). This work often calls forth other visual phenomena (dreams) as the process of accepting the imaginal realm—as begun with the help of waking dream—proceeds.

The notebook is an analog of the brain. The left column

Mar. 14, 1981 Waking Dream #2

Left   *Right*

                    Writing*   Drawing*

Figure 3.1   Waking Dream Notebook

*Left and Right and Writing and Drawing need not be included. Their inclusion here is for expository purposes only.

is the correlate of the cerebral hemisphere that mediates verbal expression; the right column is the correlate of the cerebral hemisphere that mediates visual phenomena; the vertical line down the middle is the correlate of the corpus callosum.

In conducting waking dream work, the instructor must keep his voice at an unvarying, normal, everyday level. Most people tend to let the voice drop in instructing an exploration, which can induce a deep hypnotic state, moving the explorer away from the waking level too quickly and thus away from his groundedness. The explorer must find his own pace by himself. Artificially stimulating any deepening of the experience is detrimental.

Also, the voice becomes the "voice of reality," intervening throughout the work to keep the explorer grounded in concrete reality so that he doesn't "fly" away or move into habitual fantasy. The latter ordinarily occurs when one elaborates inner life on one's own. The conditioned habit takes over and the explorer moves into regions that are familiar; hence the intrusion of the instructor's voice helps him escape the habitual mode.

The following is a detailed account of a waking dream, of the second stage described above between the explorer (E) and the instructor (I).

> The dream is one in which I'm going between two high cliffs and I'm quite safe. First the cliffs are very, very high and then, gradually, lower and I seem to be going uphill and I'm either walking or riding in some kind of conveyance. I'm alone; occasionally there are people who I do not know but who are friends. I get to the place where the road or the pathway is level with the top of the cliffs and there is a river which is frozen at one end and as I walk along, the frozen river, the frozen trees, the snow and the ice gradually disappear; and I get to a place where it's green and the river is flowing freely. Then I get to a place where I want to go on and I wake up. That's the dream. I'm enjoying it, I feel I've gotten some place and I want to go farther but then the alarm rings so I have to get up. I think the place I get to just before waking is most significant. I get there by moving along the stream.

After achieving a relaxation state with the help of the instructor, the explorer returns to the dream.

E: I'm sitting by the side of the river and listening to it. It's making a lovely, curling sound. I watch and I see a shiny, polished bed of the stream, the water is going over that, making lovely sounds—almost musical—it is musical but it doesn't have any special tune.

I: So listen closely to the sound and be with the sound and know that as you're with the sound that you find yourself more and more there and that you're more and more a part of this entire scene, that it more and more belongs to you, that you will participate in the sound of the stream. Is this a freshwater stream? (Here I bring the person's senses into the waking dream.)

E: Yes, and the sun just came out.

I: And where is the sun in relation to you? (I place the senses *there* again.)

E: To the right. (Position is important, and will be described later on.)

I: So you see the sun and feel its warm rays. As the rays of the sun shine on you, you find yourself feeling more cleansed, more purified, more relaxed, and more strengthened. Go to the stream and kneel down by the stream and take the nice, cool, clear, crystal, calm, flowing water and wash your face with it; knowing that as you wash your face with this flowing, clear, clean water from the stream you are washing away all the impurities from outside your body. And then take the cool, clear, clean water in your cupped hands and drink the water very slowly, knowing that as you drink it slowly that you're washing out all the impurities from inside your body, so that you are cleansing yourself outside and inside. Tell me what happens to you and how you feel. (Purification and cleansing have an important place as a preparation for journeying or initiation in many traditions around the world.)

E: Warm and comfortable. It tastes fresh. It practically tastes like icy cold without the ice in it. I seem to be getting up and walking, walking along the river, which is widening out.

I: Tell me what you see and how you feel.

E: I can't see the bottom any more, although it's still clear. I'm walking into the water and it's quite deep.

I: How do you feel?
E: Comfortable, It's a little bit cold because the water is cold, but not chilled. It feels fresh. Now I'm beginning to swim. I swim to the other side of the stream. Somehow, I've left my clothing somewhere.
I: Tell me what happens on the other side of the stream.
E: I'm lying down in the sun and enjoying it. Relaxing, feeling at peace. It reminds me of a tropical island now; it seems to have changed from a stream to the ocean and I'm on the beach.
I: Do you see tropical trees?
E: Yes. Palm trees—coconut palms. There are people there.
I: Can you describe the people that you see?
E: Hawaiians or Tahitian people. Balinese, but not Balinese from the present. Balinese from before the white man came. They're warm, friendly, relaxed. They're greeting me. I'm greeting them.
I: Do they look friendly?
E: Yes.
I: Tell me what they're wearing.
E: I don't know. They're half dressed, sort of. It seems natural, either leaves, cloth wrapped around—flowers.
I: How do you feel?
E: Good. I'm going home with them.
I: They're taking you somewhere?
E: Yes. Home. Their home and my home, although I'm the visitor. I'm no longer the visitor. I have a feeling of peace, pleasure, dancing, music. The sun is shining but it seems to be evening at the same time but the sun is still bright. The water spreads out to the horizon. It's just beautiful.
I: Can you describe the place to which they take you?
E: It's like a hut with a raised area in the center. It's almost like an altar in the center, with flowers and a stoop, which doesn't fit there but it goes.
I: Can you smell the flowers?
E: Frangipani, they're red and pink with touches of gold and green leaves that they're sitting on. They've been plucked, most of them, but some are growing around, but they've been plucked and put on the altar but they're still bright and shiny—not shiny, dewy—and at the center—there's a woven plate with fruits and more flowers. It almost looks like it's a celebration of life.

I: How do you feel there?
E: At home is the best word I can use.
I: Part of it?
E: Yes. We seem to speak the same language without talking. There's no talking, a nonverbal communication. We're flowing.
I: Just their actions, you mean, and the way they are?
E: Just the way they are.
I: So what do you do?
E: Eating some fruit. Drinking some fruit juice.
I: How does it taste?
E: Good. I wish I could have some really. *It is real though.* I can taste it.
I: Describe the taste.
E: Tart and sweet.
I: So you know that as you taste it, that tart sweet taste, *that you're a part of that place.* And you know that as you drink that it refreshes you and gives you more strength.
E: It's a celebration of life and death and rebirth. Here is the river again, on the island.
I: And where are you?
E: I'm standing with them by the side of the river and we are burning some kind of fabrication. It's as if I'm burning me too. (The term *fabrication* is not interpreted.)
I: So watch the flames. See that burn and tell me how you feel.
E: I feel a warmth in the flame. It's a little bit frightening but I don't want to stop.
I: Is there anything you need to do by the flame?
E: It's a flame I have to walk through or go through or experience.
I: So tell me how you feel.
E: Scared and anticipatory. I'm reassuring myself that I'll live through it.
I: Is there anyone there that you need to turn to or to ask for reassurance—any one of the Balinese?
E: They're in it with me.
I: They're in it with you? How do they look?
E: Each one is discrete and separate. Each one is going through their own ablution—fire. Somehow the feeling of blueness seems to protect me. It doesn't mean I don't have to be burnt but it's a feeling of I'll be like the Phoenix, I'll be reborn.
I: Tell me how you feel.

E: Scared and anticipatory.
I: What happens?
E: I'd like to run and I'm staying there. The fire is getting bigger, all encompassing.
I: Do you wish to not continue?
E: No, I can go through with it.
I: So describe what happens to you and what you see, and how you feel.
E: Everything is black and red. I feel there is some blueness left but that too is being burnt away. It seems as if I'm just floating, not me but my body—everything tangible, not me. When I say me, the inner me, the core. *That* is intangible. The spirit goes on; the body is burning up.
I: So you see your body burning up, knowing that there's more than your body, an intangibility. So tell me what happens and how you feel.
E: My body is gone but I feel nothing. There is no pain; some fear still. A wondering is coming on. What will it be like? There's a great big tree.
I: Describe the tree.
E: One side is green and one side is dripping with dead moss. It's the world tree.
I: And where are you in relation to it?
E: Looking at it and moving closer. Walking towards it. Walking without moving my feet, though. There's some kind of traction and I'm moving through the air towards it. Toward the center of it.
I: How do you feel?
E: A oneness with it.
I: This is your tree. It belongs to you.
E: Not to me only, to everybody. It's the beginning and the end.
I: Tell me what happens.
E: I merge with the tree and I'm the tree. And here come the others merging with the tree. The tree takes up the whole space. Nothing else, because everything is in it.
I: Tell me how you feel.
E: Good. Relaxed. Comfortable. Neither cold nor warm. Spiritual, somehow. Flames of color are coming in, blues and golds and greens, no pastels, bright colors, and they come and they go, like waves.
I: Very vivid?

E: Very bright colors, the kind you thought would ordinarily clash but they don't. There are a few pastels coming in now.
I: Tell me how you feel now.
E: Smiling. I can feel a little bit of *strain in my back* [my emphasis; time to come back], the middle of my back. The rest of me is relaxed, comfortable.
I: So now, you leave this tree, knowing that it's yours and everybody else's, and that it belongs to you and everybody else, the world tree, and it's yours to come to whenever you need. This is your place. And thank the Balinese for bringing you there. And say goodbye to them and leave this island very quickly and find your way back to the point at which you began this exploration, seeing everything with a new perception. Let me know when you arrive back at the point at which you started. You are coming back from the island, through the ocean, into the stream. You swim across the stream.
E: Find my clothes.
I: Yes.
E: Put them back on.
I: Yes.
E: I do it with regret.
I: But knowing that this is a place that you can always come to since it's your place and your existence and it's always there for you. You come now to find yourself leaving that place and coming back into this room, and you're now back in this chair. In a moment I'm going to ask you to open your eyes and see yourself in the tree, experiencing the merging with the tree as you experienced it there with all the feelings that you experienced, and those beautiful colors and all that you saw there. And don't speak. You will see it on the white wall opposite you. So, open your eyes and see it there and don't speak. (There is silence at this moment.)

And now, as the image begins to fade, you find yourself coming back to the here and now, coming back feeling refreshed, renewed, rejuvenated, like a new person in mind, body, and spirit. And you feel your feet pressing into the rug and your whole body feeling heavy, your shoulders feeling heavy as though there's a weight pushing down in them, and your hands feel very heavy as they press down on the arms of the chair. And you find yourself breathing evenly and regularly, as you find yourself coming back to the here and now, completely awake, alert, attuned, and aware of all that's going on around you and in you: coming back feeling calm, peaceful, relaxed, full of energy, with a sense of unity and harmony about yourself inside and out. As you come back to the here and now feeling calm and peaceful, feeling all the tension going out of your muscles, breathing evenly and regularly. Now you can speak if you'd like to.

E: I was thinking when you were talking about it that I could draw it, but I'd be hard put to write it because there's too much to write. Even when I was talking, thinking back, there was like a shorthand that was going on.

An example of a patient who successfully completed the course of waking dream therapy is case #15, a man who had previously undergone 17 years of psychoanalysis because of anxiety, phobic symptoms, and, despite enormous talent, an inability to perform satisfactorily in his chosen area of endeavor. This man worked in the visual arts and had achieved national prominence a dozen years earlier. Since that time, he constantly antagonized his peers and insulted those who respected his work and sought to employ him. He was irritable and irritating. Besides being chronically anxious, he was also fearful. He was unable to take an injection or have his blood drawn. His career was on the verge of collapse and psychoanalysis had not helped him. He came to me because he was desperate. He did not want to work on his fears, which he felt were irremediable, but wanted specifically to save his career.

During his course of treatment, he consistently came back to feelings of rage, often concretized in his waking dream work by his meeting large hairy monsters with frightening eyes, gargoyles, or giants. He would respond to these encounters by taking a sword and slicing the creatures into bits. Even in the most benign, pastoral of waking dream settings, some foreboding monster would appear who had to be slain. If he had a companion, perhaps a family member, that person too would metamorphose into a monster who had to be sliced up. He began to regard his right arm as a destructive weapon, which made it difficult to use this same arm in creative work.

At one point about midway in our work, I accompanied him in a guided exercise (his choice) in which I surprised him (my choice) by suddenly turning on him and slicing him up with a sword. I then asked him to put himself back together again in a new way. This event marked a turning point in his struggle to free himself of his paralyzing behavior.

He began to recognize that he could no longer trade on his past reputation and that he had to produce in the here and now. Much of his rage was predicated on his belief that his past reputation should accord him great acceptance now. Eventually he experienced a waking dream in which he travelled by raft on a river, encountered a giant black bear which he met without fury, and explored a valley in which he uncovered a hidden treasure which, he was told, belonged to him. He took a pearl with him before returning from the waking dream journey. Following this I suggested to him that he go back briefly each morning for the next three weeks (3 has the meaning of synthesis) find his pearl, and look at it for a few seconds with the intention that he was finding the treasure hidden within him. The whole experience was to take no more than one to two minutes. This sort of daily exercise following waking dream is characteristically done as a means of reinforcing the significant discovery of waking dream experience. It is done routinely during the course of waking dream therapy.

Following this work he was hired for filming along a similar river. This work went very well. He was able to pay attention to his creative efforts and his self-confidence built markedly. As he felt better about himself, he became more congenial with his co-workers. He was able to complete his assignments to the satisfaction of his employers and he was able to stop insulting them and was more able to see their needs.

From this point on his career took a sharp turn upwards, and a two-year follow-up found him functioning in this same creative way. A four-year follow-up showed that he was still functioning at the level he achieved at the conclusion of waking dream work. His career was moving along smoothly and he considered his imagination work to be instrumental in his turnabout.

Within the actual journey itself, there are many principles that can assure a fruitful outcome. One fundamental principle is that in the spatial realm the therapist *gives instruction throughout the trip.* Instruction of various sorts exists in all forms of therapy, usually expressed as the conditions one is to follow at the outset of therapy to ensure a progressive movement (Epstein, 1976). Sometimes the patient is told what to do: "free associate," "don't act before talking about it."

In the phenomenology of space, the therapist does not remain a therapist, but instead becomes an instructor who accompanies the explorer. The explorer may encounter many dangers on his journey. Just as when we are in a foreign country we want a guide to point out what is of interest and also *what to avoid,* so we want this kind of relationship in waking dream too. The traveller can wander off, he can get lost, he may go too quickly, he may love so much what he finds that he does not want to return, he may become frozen and unable to move. Any possibility can occur just as it does in the action of everyday life. It is incumbent upon the instructor to provide the direction of movement, occasionally indicating what will be found and often advising about what to do with what is found. Often some instruction may be required *after* the explorer discovers, encounters, or finds something, or if the searcher requests it, or if he is heading toward a dangerous territory.

A depressed person may very quickly find a tomb or crypt that is dark and foreboding. At the outset of work with such a person, it may be unwise to let him enter this space quickly since the experience could be overwhelming or more powerful than he is prepared to encounter.

In the domain of primary spatiality, the holographic sphere, care must be maintained because of the potency of these experiences. Adventurous explorers will often go into these depths precipitously and may suffer unpleasant consequences as a result.

It is very important not to mistake this kind of caution with authoritarianism, which all too often grows out of the psychotherapeutic relationship of therapist (doctor)–patient. The inherent hierarchy assigned to the roles labelled therapist and patient contains within it the seeds for authoritarian abuse. These labels assume that one person has something to give and one has something to get. One takes the role of omnipotent provider and the other of helpless, dependent consumer.

Phenomenologically based therapies try to undo that artificially created hierarchy by carefully avoiding authoritarianism and that dichotomized relationship. In waking dream, there is no artificially constructed "transference" relationship. The course of treatment does not depend on the evolution of such a relationship. The instructor has no "special knowledge," nor is he made into a special image. His presence as *who he is* in the present moment serves to enhance the healing potential of the journeyer.

By healing I mean the harmonizing and balancing of the rational and nonrational processes of human existence, without prejudice, such synthesis creating a feeling of unity and wholeness with respect to oneself and the things of this world.

The journeyer finds the healing impulse through his own active effort without the instructor's *interpretation* of what is discovered. The instructor may, in fact, dissuade the voyager from interpreting what he encounters. When the therapist offers interpretation or explanation, he may be intruding himself into the patient's life, thus setting up the medium in which "transference dependency" grows. On the other hand, he may remind the journeyer that this is phenomenological work, meaning that one lets what is encountered speak for itself as what it is.

From the directness of the encounter comes the recognition of one's being. If the patient persistently intellectualizes, he hasn't moved very far from his habitual stance and has not entered the imaginal realm in a meaningful way. The instructor cannot further healing by offering interpretive explanations to the explorer. Such behavior restricts the possibility of the searcher's discovering for himself and fosters his dependency. It also interferes with the experience that works inside the individual to promote growth and transformation.

Instead of interpretation, the instructor offers *intention.* Intention is knowing in the context of exploration. It gives an inner directive plus a direction, suggestion, and permission to the explorer to accomplish what he must for his own development. He is not told what he will find, feel, or experience, but only that the possibility to do so exists. The most convenient way to frame this is by using the word *know* in the way to be described just below.

Following the induction, at the outset of the *going* phase, the explorer is told the purpose of the *exploration.* This purpose concerns either the patient's goals in treatment or the continuing exploration of a track already begun within the waking dream context. For instance, someone who wishes to overcome depression would be told something of this sort: "*Know* that as you pursue this imaginal exploration you will find what you can do to control your depressed feelings." Or in the case of someone fearful: "*Know* that as you pursue this journey, you will find what you can use to fight your fear." These intentions can be expressed in one's own style, and I hope others will find their own variations that act in the same way. However, the use of the term *know* (not to be stressed by voice change) is very important.

The importance of this experience is what the patient *sees* about himself and then knows unshakably. What is discovered is genuine *insight,* which is then brought to bear on everyday experience. The action contains within itself the healing potential. This insight (seeing in) allows the patient the freedom to reverse tendencies that have been habitual and automatic. This reversing *is* the healing moment. It is here that the searcher realizes that he has the capacity for effecting an action that will lead to his own healing, growth, and transformation. He no longer feels that he is the unfortunate passive recipient of all that befalls him, but sees that now he can *actively* create his own experience. He no longer needs someone else to *do* something for him.

The images that the explorer actively recreates, after discovering them holographically, are the concretizations of his feelings. One patient visualized despair and hopelessness as a vacuum in the sky. Another patient said she felt "grim." When asked to visualize this feeling, she described a long road, without flowers, a road she would have to travel alone, without dreams.

Because feelings do not belong in the realm of linear logic, therapists, often subtly, question their authenticity. This leads the patient to doubt his own experience and leaves him confused about what he is feeling. Imaginal work allows the patient to accept his feelings, to see what they are, and to explore them so that he can deal with them constructively. Subsequently, the explorer is encouraged to momentarily reexperience his new attitude when he finds himself entering into habitual behavior. This brief recall of the waking dream experience revises habitual patterns, old thoughts, and feelings.

Fundamentally, we are dealing with spatial realms that are characterized by extent but not by concrete matter. Waking dream is one example of this kind of realm.[6] In space, the individual needs secure anchoring lest he fly off into an irretrievable and endless orbit. The astronaut requiring anchoring while maneuvering in space or on the moon is a concrete example of such a need. The instructor provides the cues for *anchoring* the journeyer, who may not want to return, or may come to a spot—similar to what are called "black holes" in astronomy—where there is danger of being drawn in too quickly.

One man (#15), mentioned earlier, voyaged into outer space with a rocketlike vehicle, darted quickly beyond the planets, and found himself coming to a black hole. He did not wait for me, and before I could catch up to him (he had pursued this journey much too quickly from the outset), he plunged through the black hole and then exclaimed that it was "death." Following this he fell to the floor in a curled up position and began to cry, moan, and scream uncontrollably. Eventually he regained his senses, shaken and frightened. He said that after his plunge through the black hole, he was unable to control his "fit," which he likened to an epileptic seizure. (He had no previous history of epilepsy and subsequent neurological and psychological testing revealed no organic impairment.) Although he was frightened, he wanted to continue waking dream therapy.

When moving to and through the levels of reality, one must enlist the aid of an instructor who knows the way.[7] Only the seeker can experience the event and any attempt by the instructor to impose his perception of the experience on the seeker must be regarded as improper because it removes the seeker from the imaginal realm and interrupts the experiential moment, the pure instant of the present moment, with a sudden intellectual movement of thought—a movement of linear time and necessarily not of the present moment—and imposition of concrete life. During this exploration, the instructor should be recording the event in writing or by tape recording for future use with the patient.

The explorer's description *must be detailed and vivid.* This is one of the most important elements of imaginal work and *there can be no shortcuts.* It is through this vivid description that one goes by way of the senses to the various levels of imaginal reality. For the explorer, one value of vivid, detailed description lies in prompting linear thinking while employing nonlinear thinking at the same time, thus achieving a balance of these activities. It sometimes occurs, as in the previous illustration, that the searcher rushes ahead of the instructor and does not describe well. This is a sign of a wandering, undisciplined, usually confused mind. The instructor must help the journeyer to stop his habitual rushing, and he must instruct him to observe and describe carefully.

The action of waking dream is a going and a returning and is to be considered a voyage or trip. By returning along the same route, one comes back to this level of reality via a path that is now familiar, established, and safe. Explorers of all varieties—

whether they be Columbus, Admiral Perry, Jacques Cousteau, Ariadne, or Theseus—generally return by the route from which they came. In neurophysiological terms, one can imagine the journey as a new pathway being opened in the brain so that old, habitual tracks are not repeatedly followed. Rather, a new track is formed. If there are any new events on the return trip, the explorer may be asked to report them when he arrives back at his starting point.

As he returns, he is told to keep the good or positive feelings for himself; or to keep whatever was valuable to him for himself—a concrete object or a realization, advice, or answer—while at the same time rejecting whatever was negative,[8] but not before he has examined it. He also is told that whatever he discovers—places, things, insights—are his to keep or to come back to whenever he might need them.

Discussion in the succeeding session(s) should focus on the experience of waking dream. By deferring the discussion until the next meeting, the possibility of intellectualization is postponed and the full impact of the event can work inwardly, unperturbed.

The subject's response is related to the state of preparedness for transformation. Often he will say that what has occurred is quite clear and needs no discussion. But often "less" of a transformative response will be forthcoming. In these instances, it is advisable to go over the work. The seeker shares his report with the advisor,[9] who compares it with the account he has transcribed and points out at the end what the explorer has forgotten or omitted. There is neither interpretation nor analysis of what is forgotten. What was omitted is important only in that it has not been assimilated into the exterior life in the waking world. Imaginal work seeks to harmonize the interior and exterior life, inner and outer reality. By seeing what he left out, the seeker can begin to synthesize these two realms. He is thus alerted to possibilities in his life that he had previously overlooked or resisted acknowledging.

As I mentioned earlier, one can see that an event occurred

in a qualifiable spatial realm outside of linear time. The event is then placed back in time, that is, the world of linear dimensionality that creates the concrete world. The writing and drawing of the event, as well as seeing the event outside oneself upon returning, *puts the event in time*—the world of physical action. It also calls upon the person to be in the world of concrete life. In this work one must *always remain in life*. If the event is not put in time then the energy decomposes and returns back to the unorganized energy or interference pattern (see the earlier discussion of the hologram on pp. 47–49). This in turn has a physiological effect on the individual that can sap his strength and lead to apathy.

Another effect of not putting the event in time is the tendency to lose one's groundedness on the earth. The imaginal event is seen in this context as having a life of its own unrelated to the concrete world. This attitude calls the person away from living life as a human existence and leads to great vulnerability and subsequent depression.

Another effect of waking dream is the reversing of habitual reactions. For example, instead of always fleeing in terror before a monster, one stays and confronts it.

One person (case #50) dreamt of a huge living monster arising out of the water, and she fled in terror. This middle-aged woman lived a singularly lonely life. She considered herself unattractive but was usually able to attract men. These men, however, treated her shabbily and her relationships with them were all unstable and impermanent. She habitually used tranquillizers to stem her rage, usually directed toward men, and to allow her some sexual intimacy. In all her social relationships she was needy, dependent, fearful, and seemingly helpless. She came to me wanting to establish a lasting tie with a man. She had previously undergone 16 years of psychotherapy, which conditioned her to rationalize and explain her behavior as caused by her intrusive smothering mother and her detached, cold father. She lived in constant terror of intimacy. As a child she constructed a world image of herself as ugly, worthless, and unwanted. And as is usual with those who construct world images when young, she set out to prove that her image was correct. One of her pervious therapists focused on getting her to correct this image, and she met that attempt with a more fervent determination to hold on to it.

In her previous treatment, "transference" became the important issue and there she changed her image, literally, through multiple plastic surgeries. She hoped that such an expression of love would prompt her therapist to love her in return. The response she got was stone coldness. This increased her ardor and she tried to change more drastically through more surgery, which again was met with coldness. Finally her desperation ended in a breakdown and the treatment was broken off.

In her course of waking dream therapy, she reported a dream in which she fled from a monster that rose out of the water and threatened to destroy a seaside house where she was staying. In the waking dream following the night dream she returned to that seashore, and reflexively started to run away in anticipation of whatever was going to emerge from the water. I indicated that she could stay if she wished and could bring along any protective device she wanted. She elected to stay without any protection. The monster emerged in the form of a giant blond male creature. She stared directly into his eyes, and he became friendly and tame. She felt that she had overcome some great impasse within herself.

Subsequently, she said that while she was not out of the woods with regard to a lasting relationship with a man, she did not feel hopeless as she had in the past since she had seen in her waking dream the possibility of reducing the monsters and frightening qualities of men to a more manageable level. This perception allowed her to find a new way of relating to men. About two weeks after this experience she met the man with whom she established the first sustained relationship in her adult life.

Another explorer (case #86) was a woman of considerable acumen who found that she was feeling chronically depressed with intermittent outbursts of anxiety. She felt as though she were letting life pass her by. In her imaginal reality, she found a waterfall near a fresh, flowing brook. She bathed herself in this waterfall. (Water is the source of purity and strength, qualities previously unavailable to her and which she needed in order to contravene "dirty" feelings.)

This woman had been plagued by feelings of worthlessness all her life. She lived in order to fulfill this world image. She indulged in hedonism that also made her feel contaminated. She found herself easily influenced by others, and this, coupled with her own inherent sensuality, aroused in her terrible emotional conflicts. Her inherent morality fought with her hedonistic behavior. She searched ceaselessly for some means to cleanse herself, generally looking to others to give her permission to be pure. This habitual searching was fruitless and frustrating. She had difficulty finding moral models: her parents lived hedonistically, and it did not occur to her, as it does not with most people, that she could be her own model. When in a guided exercise she was put in touch with a source of purity within herself, she could cleanse herself of guilt in her imaginal existence. As she was now able to find the possibility for purification, so her feelings of depression, tied as they were to feelings of guilt, could be cleansed (i.e. wiped away) in concrete reality. The possibility seen in the imaginal realm gives hope for an option previously considered unavailable. This event gives one a push to change.

And so it was with this woman. She was told to begin each day by cleansing herself for one to two minutes at her waterfall when she felt the need to. In this way, the experience that belonged to her was made a permanent part of her everyday life. Her social anxieties, tied as they were to her moral concerns, lifted considerably. She became creatively involved in an organization giving care to underprivileged people. Her marriage, which was suffering in part because she felt unworthy of her husband, solidified as she felt more worthwhile and less plagued by her past indiscretions.

These examples can be multiplied by the dozens. But the

point is that waking dream opens new pathways and permits the creation of fresh action. The subject's own effort helps him keep to the new pathway instead of following his habitual tracks. He finds the means for this reversal in his own will, which is a movement of energy actively asserting itself through man as its vehicle. The energy that has habitually asserted itself in one direction is shifted to a new direction. It is this shifting process that opens up new possibilities for fulfillment and for an overcoming of habitual tendencies. The action of this reversing is the healing moment. It is here that the explorer (#86) realizes her capacity for effecting an action leading to her own healing, growth, and transformation. She no longer feels herself as a passive recipient of what befalls her (see p. 83), but can now actively create her own experience. Her intentionality (in the sense of inner motivation) is the agent of this will, and her human existence is the field where the intentionality is directed.

The person who practices waking dream is not always aware that he can actively use what is discovered in daily life. A painter (case #90) found a band of eagles in her imaginal work. One eagle swooped down. She climbed on and soared into the sky with it. She felt exhilarated. Following this work she soared each morning for one minute on the back of her eagle. She had found her eagle nature and this resulted in a dramatic lifting of her chronic depression with a concomitant burst of creative energy and a transformation of her style of painting. Before she had painted abstracts in blacks and greys. Afterwards, she began using bright colors with motifs representing life and energy.

Ordinarily, this painter who soared every morning would not be aware of the benefit of using this technique daily. It is part of the advisor's job to alert the explorer to engage in such daily practice. Most people are not aware that a transposition from the imaginal to the concrete realm can be effected. Our cultural conditioning denigrates the genuineness of this sort of activity. But the effect of incorporating the imaginal experience into everyday life allows one to alter the habitual approach to life, and to keep the link between the two realms of existence alive. The painter's soaring like an eagle reminds her of the possibility—offered by the imaginal realm—of the freedom to overcome some of what had kept her perennially bound up. She is also told that if she finds herself falling into depression she can reexperience "eagleing."

I must repeat that in subsequent discussions about waking dream work, the advisor must refrain from offering interpretations or explanations of the experience. Instead of looking for antecedent causes, the focus is shifted toward understanding the signs about the movement of one's life. That is, the waking dream provides pointers to which attention must be paid about the conditions of one's life. One attempts to capture the pure instant and to live in the present moment. Living in the present moment *is* life.

It is important to remember how the phenomenological approach to existence(s) relates to imaginal work. To begin with, the phenomenal event is understood to be a concrete reality. *The event is never metaphorical.* (Indeed, no experience, i.e., action, is metaphorical.) *The experience of waking dream and night dreams are real events that are lived by the human being.* Since we are attuned in the waking state to live in accordance with the rules of rational thought processes and its attendant syntactical rules, we cannot ordinarily apprehend what is revealed to us in these nonrational events. There are three requisites for making the connection between the two realms (1) we must be cognizant of the signs embedded in the imaginal event; (2) we must live the symbol in everyday life; (3) we must translate the events of the nonrational realms into concrete action in everyday reality and fulfill the possibilities for our existence. The concrete event denotes here the possible potentials (i.e., existences) that are either open to us or that have been closed off to us.

A young woman (case #59) climbed a hill and found a group of what appeared to be angels sitting in a circle playing instruments and chanting. She was invited to join the circle. While joining in she suddenly saw the three "mother letters" of the Hebrew alphabet: *aleph, mem, shin* (אמש). These letters had great power and meaning for her then (although she had no current connection with Jewish life or Jewish studies) and she brought the feelings back to her waking life. In Judaism these three letters are the primary building blocks of creation (P. Epstein, 1978); in fact the woman felt in contact with her creative potential, which had been closed off to her for many years.

She did not live in America and could only come to one session. She wanted to find a way to use her creative abilities. Her training had been in therapy and theater arts but she was afraid that she would be inadequate in working directly with someone who wanted help. She had confined herself to a routine office job and now felt stagnant. Following her waking dream experience she gave up her office job and took on direct counselling. She made herself a talisman by drawing the Hebrew letters as a triptych and hung this in her home to remind her of her potential and intention for such creative work.

Both participants must pay attention to the signs that appear in imaginal work. The signs are used as a guide toward the conduct of one's life through action. Signs are not used to give interpretations about why someone is the way he is, but rather to indicate a course of action he is to take in his life. By taking action, he learns far more about himself than he would by acquiring interpretations about his actions. Only by living in an actional sense can one fulfill the possibilities for one's existence.

It could be argued that even with the understanding of the signs a person would compulsively repeat old habitual actions because he does not know the cause of his repetitive behavior. By understanding signs, as they are recognized and encountered instantly, in the immediacy of imaginal work, a flash of insight occurs, exerting a propulsion toward new action. Such insight and new action obviates the need for knowing the cause of repetitive behavior. The old behavior is readily recognized as unnecessary and is discarded. My experience and observations as a subject, as an instructor/advisor, and as a supervisor of other instructor/advisors in waking dream work has borne this out.

As waking dream therapy proceeds, the instructor/advisor role diminishes; there is less to do in the way of directing movement or warning about danger. There are usually two major reasons for this: 1) the traveller becomes more accustomed to the imaginal reality and is more able to direct himself; and 2) *he often finds his own internal instructor.* This instructor can be a human, animal, or mythical creature, or ancient religious being (including angels) who conducts the voyager to where he has to go, answers questions about what the traveller needs, or gives the traveller some item (e.g., a gem, a book, wand) which he can use to help him find something he needs, or to remind him of something he needs to keep for himself. The item has been termed *amulet* or *talisman*. It is an emblem of some feeling or attitude one must acquire and make part of one's personality. It is essential, when such an object is acquired in waking dream, that in the following waking reality, a similar object be obtained and worn or kept in one's possession. In this way it serves as a reminder to the wearer of the feeling to be kept and developed. It is the advisor's responsibility to advise the journeyer of this necessity. It is also necessary to indicate to the journeyer that he *go* to some place in waking reality that corresponds to what was explored in the waking dream experience if that place is concretely accessible. Whether the explorer follows the suggestion or not is purely his own choice.

This inner instructor, who is a different part of the self and who has been discovered in imaginal reality, serves at least four different functions which should be conveyed to the traveller: (1) this inner instructor belongs to him and is part of him; (2) the inner instructor is real; (3) he can be called upon whenever needed to provide answers to problems or dilemmas; (4) what the inner instructor provides for the voyager is to be applied and carried out in the world of concrete, waking reality. As a different part of the self, he may point the way to what we need at the moment to push ourselves along. The inner instructor must be found by the explorer and not suggested by the instructor.

The participant usually needs to *prepare* himself for contacting a different part of himself by first finding and securing what he needs. When doing imagery work, the potential voyager must be gauged in order to see whether he is ready to undergo it. He must not be forced into this work until he is willing; he may have to develop trust in the instructor or overcome his habitual skepticism.

Another aspect of *preparation* involves the recognition of one's own contribution to what befalls him. That is, the individual must become aware of his responsibility in shaping the events that he ultimately comes to see as disturbing and inhibiting. If someone is not aware that a distortion exists, it may be premature to ask him to use imagination to help correct such a habitual distortion.

A young man who experiences difficulty in relating meaningfully to women fails to recognize at the outset of his treatment that he has behaved obnoxiously around women he likes. His ruminative complaints are that women do not care about him or that they only want to use or hurt him. Since he does not recognize his own contribution to the problem, it would be inappropriate to ask him to do a guided exercise or waking dream for finding some way to correct his behavior or attitude. Instead, it would be appropriate to engage him in a guided exercise in which he sees his relationship to women. In this way, he may vividly recognize his insufferable behavior and become ready for subsequent imaginal work to correct what has now become apparent to him.

Initially this young man might write that he wants to establish closer relationships with women. The instructor might ask how his previous relationships have gone, and from the answer, determine where to start. If the young man says he is mixed up about the effect of his own attitude or behavior, the work might begin by helping him see *what* is his attitude and behavior. Or he may admit immediately that he is the cause of unsuccessful relationships. Here the work may begin by looking at *how* his repetitive actions can change.

A different preparation is necessary for those who cannot see images. Usually these individuals are highly intellectualized and may be given to compulsive or obsessional behavior. To introduce them to imaginal work, one can try to have them close their eyes, visualize a familiar locale such as a meadow, field, or lakeside, and to describe it in detail. Once the detail is forthcoming, one can go on from there to explore the terrain beyond the familiar. Another exercise for those who do not readily image is to ask them to take a red or yellow balloon in both hands (imaginally), blow it up and let it go flying out the window following where it goes.

The determination of what sorts of exercises and settings to use becomes the art of practicing waking dream therapy. I can only provide the principles underlying this work and leave the field open to each practitioner to use his own imagination for the specifics. Each practitioner should devise his own exercises based on his every day personal experience, plus what he gleans from his reading in a wide variety of areas.

For the instructor/advisor to practice waking dream therapy successfully, he must bear in mind five conditions:

1. not to impose his will
2. to avoid preconceptions
3. to avoid skepticism, personal emotional responses, and judgments
4. not to use the first person plural (i.e., "we")
5. keep the description in the present tense

In my experience, waking dream therapy achieves results within three months to one year with one or two sessions per week. If the person is strongly oriented toward focusing on his content of thought and has come expecting to analyze his existence, then a period of preparation is usually required. Often this explorer must develop trust in the instructor. Generally, the instructor emphasizes the explorer's possibilities for fulfillment, and can initiate some preparatory imagination work at the right time (to be described on pp. 117–119). These processes often stimulate the occurrence of imagery and provide motivation for embarking on imaginal work. In instances where waking dream work is begun only after a period of preparation, the therapeutic results take place within two years, employing one or two sessions per week. The decision on the number of sessions per week is a combination of judgment on the instructor's part and motivation on the explorer's. In some instances, an acute emotional situation, for example, the explorer may have to come more than twice per week.

Waking dream cuts across all diagnostic classifications. There are no contraindications for its use. The concern in phenomenological work is the *process* of unity, harmonization, and balance, *not the label* to attach to a person. To the phenomenologist, psychological categorization is not of essential importance, particularly in deciding for whom waking dream is warranted. The necessary requirement for reaching the imaginal realm from the phenomenological perspective is the presence of the right cerebral hemisphere. And thus, the group for whom the method of waking dream would be suitable is really any person motivated to do so. In waking dream therapy the criteria for selection is not relevant so much as the instructor's ability to select the appropriate exercise for the explorer.

Notes

1. Dan Brown, a clinical and research psychologist, made an in depth comparison of waking dream, hypnosis, and mindful meditation while working at Cambridge Hospital in Massachussets. He discovered that waking dream is a distinct state from hypnosis and mindful meditation. Waking dream has its special characteristics distinguishing it from the

other two at levels of significance ranging from the p<.01- p<.001 range. The full description of the study and its implications will appear in a special summer 1981 issue of the International Journal of Clinical and Experimental Hypnosis devoted to altered states of consciousness.

2. Some investigators (Kleitman, 1963; Mundy-Castle & McKiever, 1953) have been unable to discover discernible differences between the waking and hypnosis EEG.

3. Closing the eyes shuts out external stimuli and allows one to enter more readily into the experience of waking dream. Certain explorers who are given to excessive ruminative thinking, labile emotionality, or homosexual orientation, may be particularly concerned about closing their eyes. If they wish, they may keep their eyes open. Generally, once these individuals begin to trust themselves, their experiences, and the instructor more, they will be more prepared to close their eyes.

4. This *know* will be explained when the second stage of the journey is described.

5. The restriction of physical activity is very important in waking dream because physical movement brings the senses back to the external world and away from the imaginal world.

6. The dream is another existence in which events occur, and, as such, is a spatial phenomenon. The dream existence is characterized by the nonsubstantiality of what is encountered, in contrast to the substantiality of concrete reality.

7. The Islamic theosophers refer to these realms as Absolute Matter, characterized by having form and extent, but not substance. Substance is characteristic only of concrete reality.

8. Occasionally the traveller discovers something negative and returns to the concrete reality with these disturbing feelings which will have to be worked on subsequently.

9. During the journey, the therapist is the *instructor*. During the discussion, he becomes the *advisor*. The division of roles in phenomenological treatment will be discussed more fully in ensuing chapters. The patient is a *journeyer* and *explorer* (also voyager, traveller, searcher, seeker) and thereby remains human, like the instructor/advisor, rather than becoming an object of study.

Chapter 4

ILLUSTRATIONS

Waking dream is applicable in many areas of the clinical encounter. The critical point is that regardless of diagnostic label, this method can have a powerful impact on the patient's life. No account can encompass the full experience of waking dream and no two instances of waking dream experience can replicate each other. As I have set out only to enunciate principles as broad brush strokes, the finer details are left to each individual "artist" viz. instructor/advisor who must find his own way and use his own ingenuity. The clinical illustrations can only give the flavor of the work and outline the working principles.

The clinical approach to the phenomenology of space is concerned with the process of one's being, or more aptly, one's becoming. As was written on the Temple of Apollo in ancient Greece, *becoming is now*. The goal of assisting another human being in becoming one with his being, fulfilling his utmost potential, and carrying out his life's purpose, prompts the waking dream practitioner to look not for causal interpretations but rather to focus on the recognition of what one *is* through *action and lived experience*. Therefore, the waking dream approach is not open-ended as it is, for example, in psychoanalysis. Instead, the person is asked to focus on what he wants to get out of his work. Thus the explorer sets out to discover something essential about himself. The more specific the desire, the more directly his work goes. Sometimes what he wants to get is vague and uncrystallized. But after the first or second waking dream or guided exercise, he becomes much clearer about what he wants. As he moves on he may find this desire changing, and so he works on yet another intention. Often the explorer finds what he needs, and this recognition boosts him to a new level of functioning and understanding about himself and his relationship to life. The aim of waking dream work is to give a push to the person, getting him over an obstacle so that he can carry on his life more rhythmically. He begins to live with a new perception and with the sense that he can shape his existence. He begins to live more immediately in the present. If he should become stuck again along his way, then another boost from waking dream may be appropriate. There is no need for extensive analysis. Waking dream work is one of synthesis, which carries with it learning to *be* in the experience of life, as distinct from knowing the experience of life through causal interpretation. This technique is universally applicable. Its roots extend back into biblical times, and it has emerged in such forms as the myths and fairy tales that have shaped our culture.

A young artist (case #90), mentioned earlier, found her creative energy blocked and was frustrated and depressed. In a waking dream experience, she ascended a golden ramp that turned into a steep path with three rungs that were very far apart from each other. When she arrived at the top, she saw far off in the distance white and pink mountains with a flat lake in front. She then found herself floating off the top of the ladder above the lake and the mountains. "I become like an eagle soaring and floating about, high, high in the air. A marvelous feeling." After returning, she recognized the eagle possibility of her being. She contacted the eagle potential within herself and could become united with that experience.

The potential for ascent and all the possibilities that are

inherent in that movement for her were experienced in the imaginal existence. As she was able to see a counteracting movement to that of depression (what she called a "downer") energies connected with going up were liberated. The eagle, of course, is the highest flying natural creature and thus showed her the great heights that were possible for her to attain. This woman had been greatly inhibited previously in her artistic expression. She had usually found some reason or other to intrude on her artistic work and used these other matters as a rationalization so as not to pursue her art. Naturally, she could feel nothing other than depressed because she was not fulfilling this potential, nor living up to her possibilities. Phenomenologically, when one subordinates one's own fulfillment for the sake of fulfilling someone else's needs the resulting mood encountered is depression (this is not the only reason for depression but such discussion must be reserved for another occasion). Her climbing the ladder shows the noncontiguity of space; and the entering into space occurs by floating off the ladder; and the nonlinear mode happens when she becomes like a soaring eagle.

She took further excursions aboard her eagle, which lifted the oppressive depression and brought a concomitant release of energy that she poured into her artistic work, which assumed a new and more vital direction. Shortly thereafter, the vibrancy of her new work caught the eye of art dealers and she had her first one-woman show. A three-year follow-up revealed a stabilized emotional life with continued growth and expansion of her artistic life.

An energetic and industrious business executive (case #6) who had previously gone through a five-year psychoanalysis was dissatisfied with his marital and sexual life. Although he was an intelligent and warm father, he found himself feeling markedly angry and resentful of his wife. He was unsure about how to gain a perspective on his marriage for, in truth, his wife was not incompatible or unsuitable. The following waking dream was instructive and rewarding for him.

He first discussed a night dream in which he was in a large, luxurious office with three doctors. One was very tall, thin, blond, and homosexual. One was short, stocky, and dark-haired. The third he could not distinguish. There were red drapes which he began to open, but the tall doctor did not permit him to look any further and closed them. As was his habit, he discussed his fears about homosexuality and thoughts about me, whom he related to the homosexual doctor (although I am neither very tall, thin, homosexual, nor blond). He was intrigued by the red drapes since the tall doctor would not let him open them.

In the subsequent waking dream experience he found himself at the red drapes. He began to feel very sad, and he cried. He spoke, surprisingly to him, about his mother's death. His father had told him about her death and had told him that he, the explorer, had neither gone to the funeral parlor nor to the funeral itself nor the cemetery, and he had always been ashamed of this. The drapes in the waking dream were those of the funeral parlor where his mother was lying in the casket. He could see her dead face, pallid and still. He was quite shaken by this experience.

Upon returning to waking life, he insisted that he "just knew" that he had indeed been to the funeral parlor and that he had seen his dead mother. He thought then that his father had lied to him throughout his life by telling him that he had not gone. He wanted to ask a relative about what had actually happened. If he had gone, he had to know why his father had perpetuated this distortion for over three decades, either through lying or by his own misperception.

He learned from an uncle that he had indeed gone to the funeral home and to the cemetery and that his father, because of his own emotional distress, had forgotten this.

Once he contacted the actuality of his mother's death, and no longer feeling it necessary to participate in his father's distortion, he could loosen the ties toward the emotionally significant deceased person, go through the usual mourning process of this particular culture, and then turn his energies toward his current emotionally significant relationship with his wife. He was much warmer toward his wife and found himself much freer with her sexually. He attributed the change to his looking concretely at his mother's death. He came into direct contact with the jealousy he had experienced continuously since childhood, first of his older brother's relationship to their mother, who adored the brother, and currently of his stepson's relationship to his wife.

Subsequently, he reported a dream in which he and his wife were in an all-white cabin at a place resembling Cape Cod. Somehow he was separated from her and found himself looking at the cabins that surrounded his. They were all dirty and squalid and contrasted with the whiteness of his. Upon awakening, he realized how much he had been demeaning himself and inappropriately holding his wife responsible for his own behavior.

After the dream, together with the preceding events, he was able to take responsibility for himself, consequently stopping his self demeaning attitude, and finish his treatment feeling as though he entered adulthood with what he considered to be a highly successful resolution of the marital and related sexual difficulties for which he had entered treatment.

Another man (case #42) complained of persistent difficulties in becoming close to people and forming intimate ties because he was intimidated by someone else's aggressiveness, intellectual prowess, or creativity in his field. He reported a recurring dream which graphically illustrated his predicament: "I am in a southwestern setting. I am in a ranch-house that seems somewhat run-down. I am on the floor and a man, dressed like a cowboy, has his foot on my chest, holding me down. He menaces me with a fist, and says to me, 'You're going with me into the desert.' I don't want to go with him but I am afraid. And out of the corner of my eye I notice an old woman in the house. I surmise that she must be the mother of the family."

I indicated to him that he was to return to the dream with

the intention of facing intimidation and finding out what to do about it. He returned to the most intense point: the man who had his foot on the patient's chest. I asked him to describe the man. He said he was 5'6", very stocky with a leathery, tan-skinned face like a cowboy, and he was ordering him to come along into the desert. He felt trapped by this situation. I said that he should find a way of extricating himself. He grabbed the cowboy's foot and twisted it fiercely, sending the cowboy reeling backwards. He got up and the cowboy began chasing him around a table. The patient thus eluded capture and brought the situation to a stalemate.

I asked him to describe the room, and he described a staircase leading up into another room. I suggested that he ascend the staircase. He said there were three steps leading up to another room, which was bare, painted white, and contained a door. I asked him to go through the door, and upon so doing, he found blackness. He felt scared. I asked if he needed some light and whether he wished to go on. He said that he did not want anything and that he would continue.

He entered the darkness and found himself going through door after door. It was curious to him that he did not have to open these doors in order to go through them. It was as though he had rearranged his molecules, dissolved, and came together on the other side of the door. He descended through seven of these until he finally came to a garden.

This garden was described as a lush jungle overgrown with large, deep green leaves that permitted barely any light to penetrate. The garden was bordered by high walls that slanted outwards; as he looked up and beyond them, he saw light. I asked him to climb the wall(s). He said that he could do so without a ladder or other device because the walls were so close together that he could get traction by alternating his leg movements on each wall. He reached the top, bellied over the edge, and lowered himself down the other side with a rope and found himself standing on the sand of a beach. He picked up the sand and let it sift through his fingers.

I asked him to keep one grain in his palm and to look at

it, watching it quickly transform under his gaze (in nature sand can be transformed into pearls, by art it is transformed into glass). A small knight sitting astride a small horse appeared in his palm. The knight wanted to be placed on the beach. On reaching the ground, the knight and horse grew slightly in size. I suggested that he ask the knight's name and whether he could help the patient in his quest to find out how to combat intimidation. The knight said his name was Lothar and that the patient should follow him.

The patient was *guided,* led to a medieval-looking city that was quite small in size, where all the people were the same size as the knight. The patient became hungry, and the townspeople offered him food. He ate but felt bad because he ate in proportion to his size and would soon use up their food supply. They told him that he could repay them by clearing land so they could have more room for planting. He began uprooting trees outside the town, which was easy for him because the trees, like the people and the town, were quite small.

After taking care of this job, he asked if they could help him with what he needed to know. Lothar told him to go to the beach by the water's edge.

He did so, and there he found a beautiful boat, the most beautiful he had ever seen. It was made of natural wood, perfectly hewn, and smooth-hulled. He climbed in, hoisted the white sail and sailed off. He sailed toward the right, feeling very free and partaking of the glorious water, air, sky, and sun that surrounded him. Suddenly, a black-hulled, very large steamer came sailing by him to the left. He could see the rivets of the steamer's steel siding. As it passed him, he suddenly felt himself being lifted out of the water. He looked and saw that a winch was lowered over the side of the black boat, at the end of which was a large hook fastened to his own boat. He and his boat were being cranked up to the deck of the black boat. I told him that he might find something in his boat that he could use to cut the cable and release his boat. He said he knew that he had to face whatever was on the black boat, so he chose to remain where he was. He was hoisted on deck and encountered there, much to his surprise, a group of men reclining on pillows. They were dressed in pantaloons, silk shirts, and turbans of varying pastel colors. He was standing above them. He had never seen any of them before. He was "amazed" at what he found. He was "flabbergasted" and "never expected this."

He became indignant and demanded that they let him go —they had no right to interfere with him in the first place. They agreed to lower him back in the water, but first they invited him to dine with them. They pointed to a sumptuous spread laid out on the deck and invited him to eat. He declined their offer and left the boat.[1] He was lowered down the side of the boat by the same winch that hoisted him. I indicated that he had discovered how to face the intimidating possibility he encountered in the world and in himself.

Back in his boat on the water, he felt very free and liberated as he sailed ahead. He decided that he had no further exploration to do at this time. I said that he should then bring the boat to shore, knowing that this was his boat which he could use to explore with whenever he wished. He quickly retraced his route past the medieval town, the people, and Lothar, all of whom had grown to "normal" size.

Having taken a necessary step via his action in waking dream of finding, facing, and forcing intimidation, crystallized as the ominous black ship and the reclining men, to yield to his confrontation, this explorer was free to find another option in facing persistent affronts to his strength and courage. It is not unusual from the phenomenological perspective to find that what one has yet to master as a mode of existence is consistently encountered. It will be consistently met until sufficiently lived. Once lived and fulfilled, such experiences no longer represent a difficulty, and in some instances never occur again.

In the following weeks he reported that he faced at least four intimidating situations of the type he had been evading prior to the waking dream. He challenged a man who had been tormenting him at work for four months, and the man backed off. He brought to a head a problem that had simmered for years with his brother over ownership of some family heirlooms. He began to challenge his girlfriend when she berated him, whereas before he had always felt powerless. He was assertive when a man in a parking lot shoved him.

His relationship changed toward those whom he had previously perceived as intimidating. He began opening up to a repetitive issue that had colored all his intimate relationships with women. He had assumed that intellectual achievement was closed to him and had therefore depended on his female partner(s) to supply this deficiency. However, their intellect had intimidated him and made him feel distant from them. The waking dream experience helped to transform him from a coward into a self-confident human being.

A 67-year-old widower (case #23) came to treatment following a prostatectomy two months earlier. Seven months prior to that, his wife of 27 years died of an illness of 10 years' duration. He responded to the death of his wife with a sense of relief mingled with grief, but the experience of the prostatectomy filled him with severe anxiety, depression, and agitation. An associated symptom was a long history of drinking, which began in earnest in his early 30s and ended when he joined Alcoholics Anonymous at the age of 61. AA had helped him stop drinking for the past five years. The patient indicated that he recognized that his problems were of a long-standing nature and that the alcoholism was symptomatic. He considered himself to be superficial, having some talent which he never developed to its full potential, because he was afraid to despite his many opportunities to do so. He had established a fairly successful career and ran his own moderately profitable business in the field of advertising.

The following session occurred two months after treatment began. It shows how waking dream can help the explorer discover an essential mode of existence which has hitherto remained hidden and which in this case led to a reduction of intense troubling feelings observed by both the instructor and explorer. He began by reporting the following dream: "I was at the AA meeting hall. A younger man came up to see me and shook my hand. This man had come from upstairs where he had undergone some kind of treatment and was cured, and was quite happy about it."

He said the young man was no one he could readily place. He felt despondent after waking from the dream which he could not account for, since a good thing happened in the dream—although not to him. Although he had had a pretty good day prior to the session, he had had touches of fear. He spoke proudly about the day of the session being his birthday. He mentioned that his brother-in-law had suffered from a depression of late life, related to an unfortunate external circumstance. This brother-in-law had gone to a psychiatrist, was relieved of his depression in six sessions, and had been depression-free ever since. He recognized that his own feelings of depression went back a long time and had been present from a young age. He thought that he no longer wanted to go to the AA meetings because only "lip service" was paid to looking within oneself. He was replacing the AA sessions with therapy, where he was hopeful of learning to use the tools that could help him help himself.

The patient went on to say that he suffered from a strict conscience and that he might feel guilty about leaving AA. Because he realized that his problem was so long-standing, he did not complain that his treatment was longer than the six-weeks' cure of his brother-in-law. "Those kinds of problems need time to be worked out," he said, and he was happy about how much better he felt in the two months of treatment thus far.

He reentered his night dream, and I asked him to describe the staircase in his dream AA hall. He said there were two steps, then a bend in the staircase, ten steps leading to another turn, then three steps going to the next floor. I asked him to climb the two steps and describe his feelings. He said he felt scared. It was completely dark and he could not see anything. He suggested using a flashlight. He walked up the ten steps, turned, and quickly went up the three steps. His emotional state seemed to be building. He said, somewhat excitedly, that he was in a ward of alcholics. There were about five or ten patients, all with dirty, bearded faces and dribbling at the mouth. He did not like the scene. At the end of the ward was a man dressed in white, who seemed to be the doctor who was treating these men. Apparently the man who came downstairs had also been treated here. Behind the doctor was a glass booth. He decided to go and ask the doctor his name. He walked up to him and discovered that the man was an aide.

His attention was then suddenly drawn to one of the beds. He noticed the bedstead, which seemed to come from a time reaching back 50 or 60 years. It was elaborately marked and peeling. In the bed was a bearded man who looked haggard, dirty, thin, and wan. On closer inspection, he saw that it was his father, and he was struck by this discovery.

As he came out of the waking dream he suddenly relived the experience of his father's being taken to the hospital in the middle of the night for an emergency appendectomy. He experienced the horse-drawn ambulance clanging through the streets. His mother carried the explorer in her arms, trailing the ambulance to the hospital. He was 2 or 3 years old at the time. He ventured that he hated his father, that his father was repugnant to him.

He then experienced being at his aunt's house at about the same age. He was lying in a room with his shoe half on, half off. He called for mother, who came into the room, and he felt better. He then experienced being at his aunt's house once again at about the age of six, when his brother was born. His mother was away. He heard sparrows that were kept in a cage outside the window, and he saw the long hallway entrance that led to the apartment. He realized that when a male member of the family other than himself was away, his mother was also away, caring for them and not for him. His subsequent thoughts harked back to how he was made to feel guilty if he wanted his mother's undivided attention.

At the following session, he said that he felt very well and seemed to be much less anxious, fearful, and agitated. He talked a great deal about how he had tormented himself continuously throughout his life. He said that his conscience was constantly punishing him. He mentioned how, when he was 57, his father died and he felt glad and released.

He described a feeling of immediate insight associated with his response to his father's dying in the bed in the waking dream, claiming that the insight experience was "like holding a ping-pong ball under the water and then letting it go. You then see it pop up before you into the air, and you see this bright white ball." Seeing this ball was equivalent to his recognition of the influence his father had on his life and also the recognition of why his mother could not give him the undivided attention he craved.

In a following waking dream he saw himself in an Elysian Field among a group of white toga-clad figures who were drinking nectar. This was one of several instances where he found himself in an ancient Roman setting. Here he felt that this, i.e., the peaceful existence, was a possibility for him to attain, but he wondered if it were open to him in this lifetime. It occurred to him that this Roman setting spoke of previous existences, of lifetimes. This was an extraordinary statement for the patient since he was essentially a rationalist with no particular religious or spiritual tendencies. He ventured further to say that if he did not succeed in fulfilling the possibility in this lifetime, he knew he would in succeeding ones.

Shortly after this, he moved to another state, having abstained from drinking during the course of our work together (approximately six months).

In this case the possibilities of the past *and* present were demonstrated. This patient showed the past *in* the present as well as the potential for his own improvement by the young man who was cured in the dream.

The patient retreated from fulfilling his life because in order to live more fully he would have to acknowledge the anger, resentment, and jealousy that constituted his relationship to his brother and father. He wanted his mother's undivided attention. But to get that he would have to demand it, and he was always unable to demand what he required. His mother made him feel anxious and guilty when he demanded attention from her while she was attending to his father and brother. So he retreated from his hatred and filicidal feelings and remained forever caged, like the sparrows he encountered in his recollection.

Through waking dream, however, he realized that he could love and hate the same person, that he could feel heartbroken and mournful without feeling guilty about hating, and that he could, in addition, experience and understand the possibility for harmonizing these paradoxical feelings. The cage door opened and allowed him the freedom to fly. The patient's chronic depression lifted immediately.

The traditional hypothesis is that developing an interpretation opens up a person's mental life to further investigation. From the perspective of phenomenology, however, and waking dream in particular, to account for the presence or perception of the phenomenon by external ideas is unwarranted and draws the patient away from engaging the immediacy of his experience. Further, the immediacy of that experience brings with it all the other connected experiences of the same meaningful nature. So, in case #23, the hospital scene in the waking dream led him to "live" the connection of being at his aunt's house both during his father's hospitalization and at the time of his brother's birth and allowed him as well to "live" the many significant times he felt unnecessary guilt.

A 28-year-old professional man (case #37) came to treatment to overcome impotence and premature ejaculation. He also wanted to be able to maintain a stable relationship with a woman.

The week before the waking dream to be described, he discussed his attachment to his mother: he informed her of all his activities with women and talked to his mother frequently on the telephone.

In a session which took place three and a half weeks after treatment began,[2] he opened by lamenting his impotence and premature ejaculation, which interfered with his ability to perform properly with his current girlfriend. He said that since the discussion about his mother, after his first waking dream, his symptoms seemed to have diminished and that he had been successful sexually with his girlfriend three times over the past week. But instead of feeling joyous about his success, he felt depressed. He also noted that he had not called his mother during the past week, and that she had called him only once. When he went to his parents' house, "she didn't pressure me about my girlfriend or bother me at all about my life."

He discussed further his feelings of depression. He felt like giving up his professional career and going off to a mountain by himself to do "nothing." He thought that this was an "unrealistic" notion. I asked him what he thought was unrealistic about that. He said that a number of his friends had done that in order to meditate, but he suspected that three-quarters of them came back no better off, or were perhaps worse. He then said that he was suddenly aware of dreams he had had over the past few days:

Dream 1. I am in a rowboat on a lake, and my father is in the boat. The boat tips over and we are thrown into the water. My father disappears and I am left alone in the water. I swim around, and I finally reach the shore where my father is waiting, and he helps me out of the water.

Dream 2. I am reading the *Society Page* of the newspaper. I see a picture of my girlfriend plus another female friend who are in a nightclub. There is a man in the picture, a movie star. The girls are wearing see-through blouses, which makes me feel jealous. There also seems to be a third girl, a friend of my girlfriend's, who is also wearing a see-through blouse. I ask my girlfriend about the picture and she reminds me that I was also at the nightclub.

In discussing the dream, he reflected on how shabbily he dressed. He said that he would not wear a tight-fitting T-shirt, although he would wear his girlfriend's, which fit him tightly. He suddently recalled that at the age of four he was playing with a little girl, a neighbor's daughter, in the house. He showed her his penis. When their parents came into the house, she announced to them what he had done. He was embarrassed and humiliated. His mother became angry, while his father half-heartedly "admonished" him and gave him a kind of wink, as though condoning the activity. He thought this incident was a sign of the inhibition of his sexual impulses then, but that "it didn't tell the whole story." He remarked further that he did not like to be naked in front of women. He was also struck by his being at a nightclub and reading the society page of the newspaper, since he had never done either.

Discussing the first dream, he mentioned that his mother would become anxious whenever he went swimming for fear that he would drown. I asked him what was striking about the dream. He said "swimming in the water." I asked him to imagine himself back in the first dream and being in the water.

In his waking dream, he said the water was murky and that he did not like swimming around and wanted to get out. I asked him if he wished to explore this water before getting out. He said he would dive under the water. I indicated that bodies of water often have objects of one sort or another on the bottom that he might find interesting. He said he did not feel anxious about diving under. While under water he saw a "used prophylactic," which he picked up and brought to the surface. He brought it to shore, where he looked at it again in a different light (literally and figuratively) and described it once again as "a prophylactic."

He then said spontaneously that it was his father's, and he experienced something that occurred at the age of eleven or twelve when his father asked him to get something from the bedroom. Searching for the item, he found a drawer full of his father's prophylactics, to which he responded with "stunned surprise" and the thought: "This can't be! My parents don't do that!" He then went on to speak of this experience as the first time he had opened himself to this perception since that time. He spoke of his masturbating, which began in childhood and which had continued to this day. He was concerned with the size of his penis and was interested in watching it grow larger. He observed that masturbation was related to experiencing masculinity, and he hoped not to feel, and not to be made to feel guilty for this activity.

He forcefully and voluntarily described this feeling at the beginning of treatment. After an initial room cleaning exercise (see below), he reported a dream in which he climbed a haystack. At that time he described a "sinking feeling—like a feeling of emptiness." He described the same "sinking feeling" in the dream of the overturned boat as well as at the time of finding his father's prophylactics, and noted this similarity of reaction to these events.

The week following the waking dream saw the disappearance of the sexual complaints for which he had entered treatment. He then began to work on the manifold ramifications of his masturbatory activity, striving toward fulfilling his masculine possibilities which were concretizied in this activity. He felt great shame and embarrassment at revealing these experiences to anyone for the first time in his life. However, when I acknowledged and accepted his activity and his feelings as genuine and necessary, he experienced a great sense of relief and said that he felt more masculine. This he manifested by directly confronting his mother, girlfriend, and colleagues without shame or anxiety.

Subsequent to the waking dream presented, he had a dream about being on the steps of a building talking to someone. In his waking dream, he walked up the staircase and found himself at the entrace to an ancient Roman building. Closer inspection of the building revealed that it was a mental hospital with enormously fat people inside. He refused to enter the building but could observe them by looking through the window. In waking life, he was extremely thin, his mother extremely fat. He said that he greatly feared going crazy, and revealed that he had taken LSD in the past and was afraid that it had affected his brain. After the waking dream, he realized that he used to think that LSD led to insanity, but now saw that his fear of insanity was rooted in his relationship with his mother.

Later on in treatment he reported a dream of being in the mountains with a group of people who came upon a ghost town. He wandered away from the group and became frightened that he would lose them. While exploring the terrain in a waking dream, he discovered a mine shaft. He went inside and discovered two desiccated bodies. He saw that they were his father and himself. Then he saw a spider. He became frightened but he took the spider outside the mine in a net. He walked with it up a hillside. As he did so it became bigger and bigger, broke out of the net, reached for his testicles, and then turned into his mother. He said that he experienced his mother as a frightening spider who castrated, drained, and robbed him of his masculinity. She drained his father and was trying to drain him. He thought of her obesity and the fat people in the mental hospital. He saw that this fat spiderwoman had enormous repercussions on his freedom to form an intimate relationship with a woman, and how it contributed to his inability to decide about marriage or to love his current girlfriend.

The experiencing of the possibility of maleness and the limitations on the expanding and fulfilling of this potential was the central theme of this explorer's waking dream work.

Seeing the possibility of masculinity was discussed with this explorer who realized that he no longer needed to surrender his masculinity to the needs of his draining mother, nor was it necessary to continue looking to his father to protect him. He recognized that he was able, nay required, to take responsibility for his own development as an independent person.

At the outset of treatment, he could not perform sexually, could not consider a permanent relationship with a woman, wanted to give up his career, could not break away from his childish ties to his parents, could not express his anger, was not in contact with his feelings, and was generally quite fearful. As treatment progressed, he reversed all of this: he saved his career, related much more maturely to his parents (e.g., he stopped compulsively calling his mother every day), performed in a sexually potent way, and could transform his anger into more cooperative work with his colleagues. Subsequently, he became engaged to and married his girlfriend. His treatment concluded on this note at the end of one year.

The movement in space within the waking dream experience furnishes a clear picture of where the individual stands in life. The spatial movement is analogous to the handwriting of an individual in revealing some basic characteristics of the personality. The patient just described swam to the left out of the water to where his father was waiting to help him. Movement to the left signifies concern with the past, and his immediately subsequent report of incidents at ages 5 and 12 bears this out.[3]

As with the 67-year-old widower, this case showed the possibilities of the past and present. The man's sexual concerns were revealed. His finding and taking of the prophylactic showed at least some openness to looking at his inhibited sexual existence.

The water appearing in his dream would be experienced phenomenologically as cleansing, purifying, creative, and renewing. Water is encountered as the thing in itself. We would try to stay away from interpreting its appearance, for example, to say that water stands for one's return to a "primal pre-oedipal union." Water in this instance would be allowed to speak for itself as the substance that washes away, in this case perhaps, guilt and shame. Water ebbs and flows. It is constantly changing yet always remains the same. It is ultimately connected with the heavens, as in religious rituals. It causes things to grow forth, yet it hides much. It is connected with birth, life, and transformation.

The experienced meaning of his finding the prophylactics at age 12 also informed his understanding of early masturbation (such as masturbating in front of the mirror at age 5) and related these events to his overriding concerns about masculinity.

The experiencing of earlier existences—generally by means of memories or fantasies—is an habitual feeling. Such feeling can be defined as the movement of linear thought in time. Phenomenologically understood, memory, then, is the living of that experiential mode, and that form of living illuminates the present experience. Memory is lived in a spatial dimension outside of immediate physicality. Since no movement of energy is ever destroyed, and since all experience is a movement of energy, all exists forever. Since all experience occurs in spatiality, the form of experience exists as a spatial dimension. Therefore, memory is not something conjured up by the brain. Rather, it is a spatial reality that is lived at a particular instant and is rediscovered when it touches on some current phenomenological realm in which the human organism is living. The brain then acts to duplicate that which it discovers through its holographic tendency.

Intense and often habitual emotions can occur as a response to the action of imaging itself rather than to the content of the exploration. This response is usually anxiety or fear, which prompts resistance to doing the work, manifested as an open unwillingness to do waking dream, or as an inhibition of dreaming. Or sometimes, instead of not dreaming, the patient will want to work only on the dream's presenting phenomena, i.e., the reported dream per se without entering into it.

The coming into attunement with earlier modes of existence that was demonstrated in the waking dream experience of case #37 and case #23 is common in waking dream exploration. One explorer (case #14) discovered in waking dream a set of photographs which showed him at age one or two being held by his parents. He was smiling. In this waking dream, he found these pictures in his parents' bedroom. He suddenly knew that he had lived in his parents' bedroom until the age of two, when he was shifted to a room by himself. At that moment in the session he felt furious at his powerlessness. He knew further that his chronic anger toward his father was not related to his constant feelings of being unwanted and displaced, but rather to his feeling powerless in general as well as in his father's presence. He was "stunned" by this discovery, and he asked his parents about his childhood sleeping arrangements. Their version coincided with the waking dream.

Following this waking dream experience, his anger toward his father diminished and his work patterns changed. He was a medical doctor and had formerly functioned only as a member of a team. Now, he became the leader of several creative research projects that he initiated.

Application of the Imaginal Function

Waking dream process can be divided into three distinct uses in the therapeutic context. These are: guided exercises, waking dream therapy, and waking dream used in conjunction with traditional therapy.

Many authors have discussed varieties of guided exercise techniques (Assagioli, 1965; Desoille, 1966). I have found that developing a few specific exercises can be very instructive since the exercises can be used with large numbers of people (i.e., for various "diagnostic categories"). In general, these exercises can be initiated at the beginning of therapy in the consultative phase. They can give an excellent picture of the patient's internal face, the focus of his problem, and in some instances be of prognostic significance. For example, a woman (#7) found an unclimbable iron chain-link fence that stretched out interminably. It blocked her way. Such an obstacle did not portend a favorable outcome to our work. And this proved to be the case.

Some of the exercises I use are asking the person to clean a room or a garden; to be in a large, calm, clear open space; to be on a beach; to be in a meadow; to focus on a dot in a circle; or to find a key and with it open a door.

In the room-cleaning exercise, the subject is to imagine

himself in his favorite, significant or most currently used room. He is then asked to describe the room in detail with his eyes closed, so as to shut out the distraction of external stimuli. He is then asked to clean the room from the top down, beginning with the ceilings, then the walls (starting near the ceiling), and work his way down to the floor. As he does so he is asked to report any feelings and thoughts that occur. He should furnish himself, in his imagination, with the necessary equipment, including a ladder.

As he works his way down to the floor level, all articles encountered should be brought to the center of the room and described. If the room is a bedroom, everything should be placed on the bed, providing *it* is in the center to begin with. Otherwise, he is told that he should have a container—a valise, trunk, barrel, carton, etc. The most useful is one that he might find while cleaning up.

As he brings everything to the center of the room, he is instructed to discard anything he does not want into that container. He is to describe what he throws away. He is asked to wash the windows, vacuum the floor and carpet, clean the fixtures, and so forth, and to describe everything he does. If the subject wishes to perform other activities such as painting the walls or polishing furniture, etc., he should be encouraged to do so. When he has all of his discards in the container (if he wishes to throw out furniture, he should place it in appropriate containers), he should put what remains back in any way that he chooses.

He is instructed to take the container(s) to the doorway, and then to clean up the center of the room. After this he is asked to take the container(s) outside to a convenient location and either burn it completely or sink it in water with weights attached until it disappears to the bottom. After describing all his thoughts and feelings on watching the container burn or sink, he returns and looks again at the room, and describes how he feels. At this point the exercise ends. It should not last more than one hour.

In this exercise, as in all the others, the purpose is conveyed as an intention or direction given to the subject to indicate a connection between this imaginal work and an effect on his inner life. In the room cleaning, for example, it is useful to tell the person that he should know that as he cleans the room he is also cleansing himself. The subject is also told that anything salutary he discovers belongs to him and is his to keep for himself.

This latter direction is extremely important because of the necessity of carrying out the discovery or discoveries in the everyday world. The patient will be inclined to do this if he knows that he is in possession of some quality, manifestation, or trait that he can use to infuse his imaginal reality into everyday life. The experience of imaginal reality fuels the will to carry out what one sees about oneself.

In the flower exercise, one sits in a meadow and, usually, finds a flower. It is picked and described in detail—the color, shape, texture, smell, (and if possible, taste). This reinforces what was already begun in the induction phase, that is, the senses are turned toward the imaginal realm, and they lead the person to exist in that space. Just as our senses lead us to exist in the concrete world, so can they be put to use in the imaginal world. If one can hear the rustling of the leaves, feel the wind blowing and perhaps hear birds chirping, the auditory and tactile senses are aroused. After the stem is described, then the leaves at the base of the flower (if there are any) are depicted. Following this, the petals are described, touched, and counted. This number is significant, since on one level it can often denote the emotional age at which the individual is fixed and needs to navigate before he can continue his natural development. From time to time during the course of therapy, the number can be checked as an indication of movement in the patient's development. This is analagous to what is experienced in dreams.

For example, during the early course of therapy, one patient (case #112) reported several dreams of being in high school at about age 15. As therapy continued and he experienced movement in his life, he reported a dream of being in college at about age 20. This corresponded directly with his experience of his own growth. The emotional age in his dream life was coming closer to his chronological age. So, too, with the flower exercise, one may, for example, count 18 petals at the outset of treatment and later on count 30 petals in another flower.

After cleaning a garden (weeding, raking, trimming, etc.) the subject can plant a seed and describe the blooming of a plant or, if possible, a tree. In this exercise, it is important that the person know that he and tree belong to each other. This reminds him that he can be *as* a tree.

Whatever the exercise, it is always important that:

1. The person report what is seen, heard, and felt. (To obsessional patients, the instructor suggests a reversed order of the first two, i.e., what is heard and *then* what is seen.)
2. The exercise not exceed one hour.
3. The person write and draw the experience, always signing the work at the end, just as any creative artist does, to signify that it belongs to him.
4. It is told in the present tense.

It is not necessary to explain the significance of the numbers or the settings. Such explanations merely reinforce the intellectualizing that interferes with and reduces the power of the nonrational processes.

One patient (case #14), mentioned above, began his therapy by cleaning a room. He experienced profound sadness, loneliness, and emptiness. He indicated that he had never experienced such intense feelings and that the event stayed with him for 24 hours afterwards.

This discovery of depth of feeling is common in imaginal work. Imagination is most suited for tuning in to emotional life. Since verbal language serves a "secondary" function in imaginal work in that it is used denotatively (descriptively) and not connotatively (interpretatively), it does not impede emotional expression. The penetration of the symbol, *which is embodied as image,* and which is the function of imaginal work, liberates the emotional energy embedded within the symbol itself. Emotions experienced in this way are not habitual nor are they necessarily attached to memory. Memory and linear thought, however, are *necessarily* attached to each other as well as to the *original* emotional reaction that occurred in the past. These memories are habitual, as are the attendant emotional reactions and feelings. The emotional reactions are characteristically painful and superficial because they automatically push the explorer to evade the feeling of the present instant.

In contrast, the emotions aroused by waking dream are liberated because they are not habitual. Instead they are profoundly and genuinely related to the present moment. They simultaneously penetrate and announce the deepest parts of our being. They permit a new organization of perception that begins to forge a link between inner and outer life unavailable to habitual, memory-laden emotion. This latter state tends to separate inner from outer life for fear of encountering that which would recall memory and, perforce, habitual emotion and pain. The new organization of perception is fundamental to the healing process.

Usually a guided exercise is followed by a dream from which a waking dream proceeds. The guided exercise is the first excursion into separating imaginal reality from the external world and the dream that follows is usually unrelated to the habitual experiences of everyday life. In effect, guided exercise sets the stage for exploration along tracks removed from the logical contingencies that dominate our relationship to the world of concrete reality.

During the course of therapy, guided exercises can be introduced for specific problems that arise, or when an impasse prevents the patient from investigating more deeply. It might transpire that fear, for example, arises which must be overcome before continuing toward the original goals. A guided exercise would be useful here and could begin with an image from an earlier waking dream; or with the instructor's asking the journeyer to find fear by descending into a dark place; or if these alternatives are not available, asking the journeyer for an image that is the concretization of fear.

Guided exercise can also be used to investigate specific areas of waking dream: an area that one wants to broaden or deepen, an area that has been forgotten in the subsequent report in the notebook, an area that touches directly on the prior goals.[11] Clinical experience will show the instructor when to employ guided exercises.

Waking dream brings a recognition of what possibilities for existence are available to a person. Beyond that, waking dream permits a synthesis of thinking, visualizing (feeling), and behaving which is lived within the imaginal existence. It is this experienced synthesis alone that gives new meaning to a person's existence. He returns to the everyday world where he has to carry out this synthesis that he has lived in waking dream. Of course, the person is also free not to carry out what he has learned, but if he knows what his task is yet fails to perform it, he accrues a debt to his own existence. His indebtedness is felt as pangs of conscience. The patient is presented the opportunity to transform his existence and redefine his relationship to the world. In effect, one has the opportunity to create one's own existence by living the function of the imaginal world and shaping the forms in and as which one shall exist.

The implication is that the act of doing, which is equivalent to living, which is equivalent to becoming, is that mode which permits a human being to fulfill his potential and so ultimately to fulfill his being. Every act of doing carries with it the action of not doing. Stopping a repetitive, compulsive action is an act of not doing, which brings with it the freedom to do something else. (This idea is concretized and given expression, for example, in the Jewish Sabbath in which one is enjoined not to engage in the usual activities of the other six days.)

One of the important facets integral to waking dream experience, and to phenomenological methods generally, is that they characteristically say "yes" to life. Waking dream *gives hope* by its initial acceptance of what is. The habit of therapeutic investigation is to say "no," to one's version of reality and then to substitute interpretive, logical, "secondary process" thought as the means toward the goal of achieving an adequate relatedness to "reality." It is a test of logic, but not of life. The habit of synthetic investigation is to say "yes," to leave life in its proper place, and to leave logic as well in its proper place.

In waking dream therapy, discussion focuses on the possibilities for existence that have been explored imaginally and on those events in waking life related to waking dream. This signifies the connection between waking dream and waking life.

For example, during a lengthy waking dream exploration, one person (case #125) discovered that she was sitting under a tree wearing green pants and green shoes. She was surprised because she abhorred green and seldom wore it. In the waking dream she also discovered a room whose walls were lined with paintings, which she looked at and found to be beautiful.

During the succeeding week she made an effort to wear green clothing. She said that for about a day and a half after the waking dream event, she experienced the most profound depression she had ever known, more intense and different in quality from any she remembered in her past. She noted that in the past she would characteristically try to turn away from depression, whereas she fully confronted this one. As she did so, she found that it quickly subsided. Her next act was to enroll in the Art Students League to begin to study painting seriously. She believed that this act expressed a genuine freedom unlike any she had known before. This waking dream disclosed to her that for many years depression was a sign of her unfulfilled potential for painting. Similarly, finding paintings on the walls in her waking dream was a sign of the appropriate action for her to take.

Signs direct our interest to what is going on in the world

at the present instant. They make us aware of the need for us to act upon seeing them. They are to be read as either correctives or confirmations of our actions. They are not to be analyzed nor is it necessary to explain their existence by virtue of some other cause. The dark cloud is a sign of impending rain. Fish jumping out of a pond is a sign of an impending earthquake. Signs confront us endlessly. They are guideposts that can deeply influence our behavior. Phenomenological work pays a great deal of attention to educating the patient to recognize and heed signs. In a previously mentioned example, a patient dreamt about college, where his earlier dreams took place in high school. This change of locale is a sign to both therapist and patient of the latter's improvement. When the corrective indicated by the sign is carried out, a confirming sign of the appropriateness of the action usually appears.

The appearance and significance of signs is not a phenomenon that can be readily understood by formal logic. To apply causal thinking to the spontaneous and often poetic language of signs is to say "no" to the phenomenon. One's attitude really has to be an appreciation of what a sign *is* rather than what a sign means (in the sense of some interpretive formulation).

Signs are often disregarded because they call upon the person to correct whatever it is the sign points to. This effort may be far more than the person habitually expends; here again, we see a requirement for the exertion of will—the mode of effort or action.

In his waking dream, one person encountered mythical beasts, all of which were colored grey. Toward the end of therapy, these mythical creatures reappeared but were now golden in appearance. Here is a clear sign of his relationship to instinctual life, which is consonant with his entire being, that is harmonious (gold), whereas in the beginning it presented danger (grey). I shall come back to signs again.

The patient is asked to read his record of the experience in the subsequent session. The therapist has maintained his own verbatim account of the exploration and follows the patient's report to note what the patient has either forgotten or added. To forget nothing indicates that the subject is connected with his inner life, which portends a smoothly running waking dream experience. Embellishment of the report rarely occurs. When it does, it indicates that something occurred after the experience, probably at the time of writing. This addition usually represents a recognition about one's being. Forgetting parts of the experience shows the lack of connection between the patient's outer and inner life and points to areas that require attention. The omitted parts may indicate to the therapist what sort of guided exercise to employ so that these areas can be investigated. The guided exercise can often be devised by the therapist to meet the specific situation.

Usually, one can elicit from the patient the image to employ. One patient (case #77) described feelings of fear and loneliness that 11 years of analysis had not helped him overcome. I asked him to concretize these feelings. He described himself as a little boy of about three or four, wearing pajamas and standing in front of a cave with a black entrance. On a closer examination, he saw a little rivulet on which there appeared a gondola. At first he was unwilling to use the gondola to explore the cave, but as our work progressed over time, he began to steer the gondola through the rivulet and was surprised and gratified by his ability to guide the boat through what was formerly a fearful, forbidding, and ominous place. As he went on, he discovered himself getting larger and older. He decided to put more effort into his work.

He was a postgraduate student disturbed by the dogmatism of his teachers. Further, he saw their values as antithetical to his. He responded by provocative, almost belligerent behavior. He antagonized his teachers and the school authorities to the point of facing expulsion. His concentration flagged and his grades reflected this.

At the conclusion of our work seven months later, his work flourished. He established much friendlier relations with the staff and gave serious attention to his studies. Most importantly, he found that he could fashion his own creative approach in his field and that differing values did not necessarily interfere with learning.

His relationship with women also changed. He was attracted to independent women and this independence often conflicted with his personal needs. He would subjugate his own requirements for intimacy or understanding to the woman's needs, silently feeling angry and resentful of her. After his waking dream work, he recognized his equal right to have his own needs deemed important.

On his final journey on the gondola, he came to an open place bathed in light, in which he also bathed. He said then that he was now free to take his boat in any direction he chose. This clearly signified the end of therapy. In his seven months of once weekly sessions, his feelings of fear, loneliness, and anger lifted, and he has remained balanced after a two-year follow up.

During his therapy we did not discuss the meaning of the gondola or the cave with the black hole. Rather, the gondola was the vehicle with which he could find freedom, become transformed, and confront those habitual feelings that inhibited his development. The cave was the element to be explored as it was the repository of his habitual feelings. He penetrated this form and was able to transform his feelings, and was thus enabled to find the strength and initiative to begin to straighten out his life.

It is through the oscillation of imaginal and verbal modes, *each used in its appropriate manner,* that the effect of waking dream makes its profound impact and heals. The verbal component focuses on the signs, possibilities, and potentials offered by imagination and also confirms the genuineness and authenticity of the person's existence to him. Clinical experience and training will guide the therapist in balancing the use of imaginal and verbal work. As is the case with all psychotherapeutic techniques, training and experience are required to use waking dream process accurately. The practitioner should experience waking dream both experientially and cognitively. This is analogous to Freud's suggestion that all those who propose to conduct psychoanalysis should undergo their own personal analysis plus didactic training, before or concurrent with their practice.

THE DRAWINGS

The pictorial report complements the written because it shows the positions of the elements (figures, settings, etc.), the colors, and what may be missing from the drawing. The quality of the draughtsmanship is obviously irrelevant.

One subject (case #92) reported that he was holding hands with a woman while walking along a path. In his picture, his arm dangled alongside his body. The woman's arm stretched away from her body to hold his hand. This man did not relate closely to women and did not extend himself toward them. Just how restrained he was in fulfilling the potential of closeness with women became clear to him as he examined his drawing.

If a house is drawn without windows, one would be alerted to imprisonment, while the absence of doorknobs would signify not being able to find a way out. That is, the presence or absence of elements indicates sufficiencies and deficiencies which point up the direction of the work.

The position of the elements in relationship to each other is an indication of where the person lives in terms of his movement and freedom. Repeated experience with many different patients indicates that when figures are pointed left or moving left, the patient is turned to the past, the mother, or struggling with emotional conflicts. Movement to the right represents movement toward the future or freeing up of one's existence. Movement upwards means ascension, which is related to breakthrough or overcoming or transcending. It is a sign of strength. Movement downwards is a sign of what is dark and hidden now, and the need to move to the depths or center of oneself.

Movement to the upper right from the lower left is a sign of power, initiative, effort, will and recreating the past. Movement from the lower right to the upper left signifies absence of will, lack of effort, and entrapment by the past. This is not a favorable prognostic sign. When the figures are in the middle, are static, or are moving straight ahead, the issues are situated here in the present time. Such a configuration indicates no movement as yet, but there is building of initiative and will. Encountering an impenetrable barrier generally indicates that the person does not want to change. Movement to lower left indicates the dark recesses of the past, while movement to lower right indicates light coming out of the dark.

Color is a matter too complicated to be detailed fully in this work, and requires deeper study by anyone undertaking to learn this process (Haule, 1977). The following is a brief treatment of the relevance of color in the therapeutic process. One can begin by noting whether the colors are dark or bright. Dark, somber colors are commonly found in the drawings of those who are depressed. As the depression begins to lift, the colors of the drawings begin to become brighter, more vivid, and alive. This is a sign of great movement in overcoming the dark mood. The change of colors to gold or the finding of golden color signifies completed transformation. In general, the changing of colors indicates movement of the personality. The change from dark to light reveals a cleansing and purification of emotional life. Within the colors themselves, changes in hues and tints indicate growth. One patient (case #34) began his work in a field where the grass was a yellow-green. Later on, the grass became a verdant, rich green. He had begun his work as an apathetic young man with little direction in life. With waking dream therapy, he began to sense that he could control the course of his life; his outlook brightened and his energy increased appreciably.

Most everyone is aware of the habitual emotional valences attached to colors. These same valences hold true for assessing imaginal work. It is important to remember that no color represents just one aspect, however, it always immediately brings with it a complementary or contrary aspect. (The same holds true for language in general—no word can be used without immediately implying or involving its opposite. Every negative must have its positive, or else we could not use language at all.) So it is in emotional life: we could not know rage if we did not know joy; sadness if we did not know happiness. Therefore, it is imprudent and unconstructive to concentrate only on the negative when talking to a patient about himself. This principle applies when discussing colors. If one encounters red, it usually means anger, but it is also strength, life, and vitality. Orange can mean inhibition, but it is also cutting through, penetrating, or female strength. Yellow can reflect cowardice or fear, and if mixed with green means that one is not sufficiently socialized; but it is also openness, generosity, and intelligence.[5] Green conventionally means envy or jealousy, and deep green signifies melancholy, but it is also sensuousness, growth (hidden possibilities), and quietness. Blue is commonly connected with depression (if mixed with pink), and introversion (if it is pale or mixed with grey) but it can also be connected with reaching heights, success, peace, and connectedness with others (if it is a hot blue). Violet can be a sign of rage, melancholy about failure in love, but also a great love, beneficence, and extroversion. Grey is at once danger and caution (for example, a fog), while brown is ordinary as well as elegant—witness the offices of the top executives of most fields. The contrasting shades of white and black signify purity and integration for the former, while the latter signifies darkness, death, and dissolution.

The drawings may establish that the person is avoiding a certain color. He may dislike it and habitually avoid wearing it. A color systematically avoided is obviously significant, and it can be useful for the patient to begin wearing that color, but without an initial discussion about the relationship of the color to mental life. It usually happens that the patient finds the connection with emotional life by himself without the therapist's interjections. *Finding the meaning for himself,* as is the case in most therapeutic forms, always gives a greater impetus to the person's transformation than any other event in therapy. In all of waking dream therapy *the emphasis is always on finding the answer for oneself.*

One patient (case #63) had been in psychotherapy and psychoanalysis for 14 years. She came to waking dream therapy because she felt stagnant and wanted to work on her inability to decide how to proceed with her career in the field of psychotherapy. We discovered that she avoided wearing orange (as mentioned previously orange often signifies both inhibition and cutting through, and female strength). She had a glimmer of this avoidance but had never sought to discuss it in her previous analysis. She agreed to try to wear orange for a short time (but not always and not compulsively, for such an action becomes habit and loses spontaneity). She began by wearing an orange scarf and concurrently noticed that her colleagues began relating to her differently. They treated her ideas with more interest and respect, and in turn, provided her with ideas that she could test and perhaps adapt into new forms that could enhance her professional field.

Before waking dream therapy, she felt she was stagnating. She had been unable to summon the strength to find a creative outlet for her energies. She had habitually expected that outlets would be provided by the field itself rather than created by her own efforts. She had been ready to abandon her career.

After waking dream therapy, she worked with greater activity and initiative and accepted a position as an executive directly responsible for shaping a teaching program for young trainees in her field, a position she had long wanted but for which she had never been chosen.

Color, along with numbers, is the most condensed, vivid, and deepest symbol known to man. All people have some innate understanding of the meaning of color and its relation to emotions. The woman who wore orange, for example, achieved greater harmony and balance within herself and in relation to the outside world. Her balancing of her dislikes with her likes affected her presentation of herself to the outside world. As she presented herself differently, so the responses to her changed and became less automatic. Color seemed to produce a "magical" effect, in that it had no direct, logical explanation to account for the change.[6] Color serves as a nonverbal connection to the emotional life of the individual. As one begin to grow in walking dream therapy, writing and drawing improve. Colors become more alive and writing becomes clearer and more connected.

Blending the lexical and visual modes through writing and drawing produces a balance of linear and spatial dimensions that serves as an induction to the will through its agent, the physical body. The will leads to performance of the requisite actions (or nonactions) that bring about a harmonization of the actional with the lexical and visual, thus promoting the living in and of the present moment. There is a call from the inner event which is made external and concrete, to fulfill the possibilities, participate in, create, and experience the transformaion all at once. It is this event that demonstrates the transcending of time with its artificial functional subdivisions into past, present, and future. This event of living the transformation validates what de Lubicz (1977) has so brilliantly eluedicated in his article *The Intelligence of the Heart: An Outline of the Symbolic Method and its Hieratic Nature.*

Schwaller de Lubicz asserts that natural science cannot apprehend by its particular observational methods all of the steps, for example, that a grain of wheat follows to become a stalk of wheat. In order to know this process, one must live the function of the grain of wheat. One must participate in and experience the process of the essent (the grain) transforming into the existent (the stalk). This is exactly what happens in waking dream. One lives the transformation, the growth from developmental level to developmental level manifested to us by the change in our perception of our relationship to the world. The lexical or descriptive mode shows us our present situation and possibilities for existence in a static, concretized form, appearing in the linear language form to which we are accustomed. While the lexical mode defines our possibilities, the visual mode shows us our movement toward fulfilling the potential as well as the potential itself. *The transformations occur in the action toward fulfillment.* This event has always to be experienced "subjectively", while the outcome can be "objectively" perceived, i.e., consensually validated.

In the example of the grain and the stalk of wheat, both of these things (entities) can be consensually validated through "objective" perception, but the transformational process cannot because it occurs as a process, not as a thing (entity). Processes are not constituted of volume, mass, nor stasis. This makes them inherently nonconsensual.

As is true of most therapeutic endeavor, there is a personal, intimate, confidential, and sacred aspect to waking dream. The patient is asked not to discuss his work nor show his waking dream notebook to anyone else. This reduces the tendency to intellectualize the process and prevents any profanation by those who surround the patient.

Night Dreams

Dreaming is a commonly occurring phenonenon which is organically connected to waking dream and guided exercise as I shall show below.

Dreams serve three main purposes in waking dream therapy. The first, and most important, is to act as the springboard for waking dream exploration. The dream is a bridge between waking and imaginal life. Dreams are linked with the concerns of the person in waking life, and are connected with the contingent dependencies that are the basis of the laws dominating everyday life.[7] However, they are dominated by laws that are applicable for a noncontingent, acausal reality. Since they are the experience of the dreamer and have not been imposed on him by an external agent, the subsequent waking dream exploration is experienced as an organic whole of the individual's own experience that is linked to dream life and to waking life. In this way the dream existence related to the noncontingent sphere is expanded and deepened. The dream then leads into the imaginal reality where perception of everyday life is disaggregated, i.e., removed from the duality that governs everyday life, is shorn of its particular form, and is experienced in its phenomenological presence.

It is the unique quality of waking dream that in this state one is at once the observer and the observed, the witness and the witnessed, the experiencer and the experienced by being in and talking about the experience simultaneously. The dream has tendencies that permit the awareness of this unity. However, this awareness is not experienced alertly in the dream as it is in waking dream. In waking dream, one initiates the activity whereas in dreams, the process is usually passive. In the dream, there is no effort to arrive somewhere, to encounter a new realm, to materialize the immaterial, or to assume the vertical axis. Waking dream is an actively initiated event in which the person directs himself to explore his *thereness* and to carry it out in the world of his *hereness*.

The second function of the dream is to demostrate to both therapist and patient the *effect* of waking dream work. If waking dream therapy is taking effect, the results show up in dreams as clear references to waking dreams or guided exercises. The appearance of the imaginal within dream experience continues the process of bridging imaginal, dream, and waking life, and provides the final link in connecting the three realms of experience. The ultimate fluidity and consonance of imaginal, dream, and waking life brings about the harmonization of qualitative and quantitative experience that serves as the indicator of the success of waking dream therapy, and at the same time serves as the indicator of the termination of therapy.

A deep and sensitive young woman (case #82) was having great difficulty in finding meaning in life, despite an excellent career, marriage, family, and social life. She embarked on waking dream therapy because it had none of the trappings of "traditional" psychotherapy. That is, she did not want an analysis purporting to elucidate some meaning underlying her actions. In the same vein she saw no purpose in being concerned with her thought content or the interpretation of it. She was a highly sophisticated woman whose work put her in contact with professionals in the field of mental health. She felt there was danger in reinforcing an individual's already fragmented existence by trying to understand current behavior as a product of some other event of long ago. She understood that such efforts only succeeded in making her feel worse because they rejected her immediacy and genuineness of being. She wanted it understood that she would be accepted as she was. I gave her that assurance (as I would to anyone asking for such assurance). Her treatment lasted three months.

During the course of her therapy, she experienced a waking dream in which she discovered herself in a circus, where she transmuted herself into a clown with an umbrella that allowed her to be airborne. On her journey she discovered a fountain. She sat in the water and cleansed herself. She felt focused and experienced slow pulsations of light going through her. The light was yellow-green at the center and, in concentric order, she also saw green-purple, red-black, blue, purple, purplish-pink. The colors merged and became green, pink, and brown. Then there were brighter streaks of white light, and larger and smaller lights. There were circles of light of irregular flame; then bright blue leading to purple and green. She was outside the white light and then she blended into the colors.

I asked her to bring the colors together into some form. (I did this so as not to prolong the merging since it is difficult for the explorer to return from the pleasure of such an experience.) Her body changed into an alternation of sinking and expanding feelings. There was a sense of airiness around her knees, and her head was large as she came back to the room after the experience.

With her eyes open she saw the entire room full of color,

both the concrete objects and the space as well. She said that her body felt less distorted and less out of shape.

This woman had initially written that she wanted to be able to provide for herself the ability to understand how she could synthesize and unify the different facets of herself. Along with this she sought to develop more courage and to experience more pleasure and less internal pressure. These latter goals were really embedded in her need to unify herself.

It commonly happens that when three elements are aimed for, the second and third are intimately connected to the first —though not invariably—and are the first to be achieved, thus paving the way to the first element. The instructor/advisor should note this when evaluating what exercise to employ or where the waking dream takes the voyager. The order of focus may not be so important when two of the items prepare for the achievement of what is usually the preeminent desire.[8]

Following this waking dream, she dreamt that a next-door-neighbor was being influenced by a fishlike supernatural monster. Unusual events had taken place and the neighbor experienced great fear. The neighbor was in the process of writing a book about it.

The explorer went on to report: "I come to you and talk about the happenings. You determine that I am not crazy, except you question if I could have a delusion in one area concerning the monster. But you also realize that you no longer know what truth is and what is possible.

Several people come in to examine me, including a psychiatrist. The wife of the psychiatrist asks you if I am crazy. You reply, "no." The psychiatrist says it is not unlike the early sea monsters. I have images of early lithographs of Loch Ness-type serpents. These sea monsters came in the spring through centuries. People used to put a statue of a dragon at the head of a harbor or put a shark in the waters, but then the waters became dangerous."

At our next two meetings, we discussed this dream, in which the possibilities of growth, creativity, maturity, and freedom were all seen. She was then prepared to synthesize these possibilities and thus accomplish the major task she had set for herself in treatment. In the waking dream reported, she had done preparatory work regarding courage and pleasure. At the outset she climbed a rope ladder which had appeared in a previous dream. She came to a platform, found a rope, and swung off the platform in large arclike swings. She swung to a higher, more precarious platform but experienced a sense of balance there. The rope vanished and she saw a staircase rising from the platform.

I asked her if she wished to climb. She said "yes," and ascended. She climbed five steps. It was very high and she did not know what was up there. At the fifth step she found a tightrope going to the ground. She gave herself an umbrella with which to walk the tightrope. She found more platforms and more stairs; her balance was good; she was waving her arms; she felt in control. It became fun. And then she became the clown.

Here one can see her courage, manifested in climbing what would ordinarily frighten her, and her feeling pleasure instead of pressure. The preparation and correcting of what was lacking in terms of courage and pleasure could now be brought to bear on achieving unity.

The discussion of dreams is an excellent way to prepare the voyager for entering the waking dream experience.[9] Between the next to last and last waking dream experience of explorer #82, we discussed her night dream in terms of carrying out the potentials she came to recognize. We noted how the locus of action moved from the neighbor to her. In the dream, she found growth (spring), creativity (writing a book), maturity (facing sea monster, becoming the locus of action), and freedom (not being crazy).

After this careful dream explication, at the third weekly meeting after the clown dream, she reentered the dream to the point of the sea monster (a combination of sea monster and guardian dragon) and had the following waking dream:

The serpent is undulating above and below in the water. It is alongside the dragon. The dragon is olive green and is willowy. It has scales of overlapping pentagonals. The overlap makes them look octagonal. I am in the water alongside the dragon. The water is cool. I am with the dragon and not really separate. I am undulating in the water. I am diving underwater and I find chunks of gold with light around them in the darkness. They are square. The light comes from the greenness of the water. I am gathering the gold together and I am making a mound. The light now is less diffuse and more condensed.

I am swimming in the light created by the halo around the mound of gold. I look good. I look like a mermaid with gold scales. I move in the water and cover all corners of the bottom of the lake. I dart like a fish and feel a sense of power and quickness. [I ask her to come to the surface—vertical movement.]

I burst through the top of the water. I look like a green plant. The gold is reflected on the water and not on me. [I tell her to keep the feelings of power and quickness for herself.] My leaves are spreading out like corn stalk leaves. They are horizontal and are stretching downward. [Describe them.] They have a red flower on top. There is a cluster of flowers. I smell the fragrance of the flowers. They are tucked inside me, within myself. I am walking across the surface of the water and on my shoulders I am wearing a long swirling cape. [Describe it.] It is white, made of gauze, and very sheer.[10] [Where do you go?]

I leave the water and am walking on the beach. I see pine trees. It is very dark at the trees with light coming through in spots. I have nothing on. I feel alone as though I am the only one in the forest. [Where do you go?]

I am walking through the forest. There are small pines with pine needles. I meet a squirrel. There are white and lavender and yellow wildflowers with large leaves. [How do they feel?] They feel velvety. I see a mountain beyond the forest. The forest goes up the side of a mountain. [Go up the mountain using the moving platform of last night's dream.[11]] I'll use gold chains to hold me onto the platform. The platform is like a carpet, but of a different texture. [Where do you go and how do you feel?]

I'm leaving the forest floor. I see the tips of pine trees. The mountain is very craggy and full of snow. The "carpet" is going at a great deal of speed and is covering large areas of the mountain. I feel short of breath. [Breathe blue-golden light evenly and regularly.] I'm at the top of the mountain, in the Himalayas. It is very beauftiful and I hear the wind whooshing. There is sun and light on the tips of the mountains and shadows in the valley. The tips are golden and make the shadows shades of blue. [Note the transforming movement of *gold* throughout the exploration. It shows up in different ways throughout. She, of course, has "found gold."]

[Look in all four directions.]

"North": I have been facing there all along.

"West"—I looked there as well.

"South"—I also have looked there.

"East"—I'm not sure what is there. I'm not sure I want to look at it. I see stars in the darkness. I feel a sprinkling from them and feel better. I see the whole Milky Way. I feel the whole environment is together again and all is friendly.

[Where are you?] I am in the center of the environment. I want to stay. There is a sense of endless space going out in all directions. I want to know if there is an outer edge. [What do you do?] I send out glances, energy, and attention to the outer limits. I'm not sure there is a "there" out there.

I sense a reversal of energy. It goes out in spokes from me and returns to me. It hits me and carries upwards and I am covered with light from top to bottom. It goes around me and has substance. *I feel in the vision and detached from it at the same time, like an observer. I feel completed here.* At the water's edge I see the *entire connection* between gold, serpent, mountain, the top, and silver. [Silver was the original substance of the harbor dragon.]

I told her to keep this understanding and inspiration for herself and to return quickly down the mountain and return to the beginning of the dream. She said she experienced difficulty in opening her eyes and that she would come back gradually. She felt that her fingers were extended, but in actuality they were not.

She opened her eyes and saw the last image of the *entire connection* and experienced its attendant insight. Her drawings showed the serpent and her moving platform pointing left. At the end, when she saw the entire connection, she was at the center of the drawing looking up with her arms outstretched, with the "connection" radiating out in gold *in all directions.*

She understood, as did I. There was no need for discussion. The way was clear.

This recognition of the possibility of wholeness encountered in the imaginal experience of plumbing the depths, scaling the heights, knowing the stages in between, facing up to her instinctual urges in the form of the dragon, allowed her to translate this experience into her daily life. Whereas she had always been caught in a perennial conflict of mother-domestic homebody-housekeeper-model wife as opposed to establishing and maintaining a career, she could now bring a balance of the two into her existence.

She no longer needed to dichotomize between mother and career woman and could maintain both guiltlessly. She saw the wholeness and thus could alter her perception about herself in the world and her attitude toward the world. She reorganized her life. She had been a dance therapist and now worked with a male colleague, incorporating verbal therapy with dance therapy. She developed her own style and became her own boss. Her home life became more fulfilling to her when she found that domesticity need not inhibit creativity. A one-year follow-up revealed a maintenance of stability and the solidification of what she had attained during her work.

This woman's course of treatment embodies the natural waking dream progression: a guided exercise was followed by a related night dream which yielded the initiating image for the waking dream exploration. The waking dream then produced further related night dreams, which led to other waking dreams. This was accompanied by discussion of potentials and possibilities of fulfillment. One span of movement at the outset of her treatment began with a guided exercise of her weeding and exploring a garden, burning the trash, and planting a tree. Her subsequent night dream took place on a large green facing a lot of tall buildings that resembled a group of hotels. She entered a waking dream exploration at that green, and this was followed by a dream about a house with an archway, which she entered to begin a further waking dream journey.

If the night dreams do not relate directly to waking dream, then the subsequent imaginal work continues from the preceding waking dream. Thus the order is: guided exercise, to night dream, to waking dream; waking dream to guided exercise; but *never* an image from guided exercise to waking dream directly (because the initiating image of waking dream cannot be imposed on the journeyer).

The third function of the dream in waking dream therapy is to help gauge the progress of the therapy. Besides acting as signs about what to work on, dreams also signal movement. A patient, (case #86, described in Chap.3), was afraid of heights at the outset of therapy. She reported a dream in which she rode an elevator to the top floor of a building, from there ascended a staircase to the roof, from which *she crossed on a thin plank without fear* to the roof of another, taller building. This dream marked the turning point of her therapeutic work.

Waking Dream in Conjunction with Traditional Therapy

Both the waking dream exploration and guided exercises can facilitate the work of traditional psychotherapy. Guided exercise can be a useful consulting tool in determining the focus of a patient's problems by elucidating the area(s) needing concentrated work and in determining the type of therapy that is most helpful. In a guided exercise, one subject (case #18) found herself in a dark, enclosed closet. She had great difficulty finding her way out and eventually had to break down the wall in order to emerge. She had come to see me not of her own volition but at the behest of a family member. This guided exercise led her to recognize her need for treatment, and she subsequently chose to enter intensive psychotherapy.

Waking dream can be used in the course of traditional therapy and is particularly useful where there has been little movement in the treatment. Diane Shainberg, a psychotherapist and colleague of mine in New York, is one of several therapists who have begun to incorporate waking dream into their work. Ms. Shainberg decided to try waking dream with patients who were having serious difficulties, if an appropriate opening appeared. Her experience has been that patients respond dramatically and with changes of attitude that traditional therapy failed to produce. The following case is hers and she has kindly allowed me to use it here.

> A 23-year-old woman entered treatment saying that her obesity shamed her so that she was unable to continue her study of acting. She weighed 370 pounds and had been overweight since the age of four. In high school, she had begun to eat secretly and drink heavily.
> She was lonely because her weight isolated her but she compensated for this by becoming the acting star of her schools. In college, she played major roles in theatrical productions but when her weight topped 300 pounds, her drama coach began to insult her in class. She began to take drugs. She became paranoid and was terrified of "disappearing." She ran hourly to the mirror to corroborate her existence.
> After college she came to New York to become an actress. She was sexually promiscuous with both men and women and lived for a time in a one-room apartment with two male homosexuals whom she would watch while they made love. She had seen several psychiatrists but felt none understood her addiction to food.
> The patient came to me after deciding against a stomach by-pass operation. She told me, "I can't stop eating. It's all I have that's keeping me alive. If you try to stop me, I'll quit. Get it?" I told her that she would stop overeating when she felt differently about her life, and for three years we seldom discussed her weight. During the course of traditional psychotherapy with me, she stopped drinking, began a serious relationship with a woman, participated in lesbian theater, and produced radio shows.
> One day she began to be concerned about what she was doing to her body. She said, "My poor heart," and began to cry. She still weighed close to 400 pounds after three years of work with me and still ate in binges. We spoke of how she was choos-

ing to kill herself. Shortly after this, she described a dream in which she was in a hospital and her mother was beside her, crying. She looked down the hospital corridor and saw something dark approaching. It had globs or clots of blood flowing down it and then a cave entrance appeared in it.

I decided to try waking dream with this patient. I asked if she would like to reenter any part of the dream. She said she wanted to go into the cave but was afraid. I told her she could have any protective devices she wanted, and she chose a torch light, a pickaxe, and a hose to wash away the globs she saw moving in the cave.

After induction, the patient put on a diver's wet suit so that the blood wouldn't suffocate her and entered the cave. I asked her to tell me what she saw. She described many arteries, masses of gluey substances, jellies attached to the wall, and descending steps made of arteries. I asked her to walk down the steps. She did and saw globs of white and felt stifling heat. She then said, with deep feeling, "This is the cave of my heart." She didn't see her heart anywhere and was afraid.

I suggested she use her torch light and she said she heard a faint sound, a beating. In the corner she saw her "tiny, pinkish heart." She was disturbed that her heart was surrounded by a mess of blobs and blood everywhere.

I asked if she could hear it and she bent down and her heart said, "I'm suffocating. Why are you doing this to me, Janey. I can't protect myself. Please help me." The patient began to sob.

I asked what she wanted to do for her heart. The patient cleaned off the mess, the blobs, jellies, clots, and found a nozzle to wash it down. She said, "I'm here, baby girl, I'm going to make you all clean. You won't have to suffocate... I'm cleaning you, then I'll blow you dry so you won't be cold." She began to blow gently. I asked what she saw and she answered, "A tiny heart, red, tired, resting, too tired to talk." She said she wanted to tell her heart something and struggled to get out of her wet suit, afraid that she would faint. Then, more calmly, she said, "I'll listen, tiny heart. I'm going to come back, but now the heat is killing me." She turned to go and I asked her to say goodbye to the heart. She did so, crying softly.

Then she panicked, afraid that she couldn't climb the stairs because she was so tired and afraid and sad. I suggested she use her torch light and with it she reached the hospital corridor again. She turned around and said to the heart, "I won't forget. I promise."

It has been several months since this waking dream. The patient has lost 30 pounds and has "not been able" to overeat. She is tempted but does not eat. This is the longest she has ever gone without overeating in 20 years. She describes her body as exhausted and remembers that her heart is vulnerable. She binged once but threw up immediately, crying and saying repeatedly, "I didn't forget. I didn't forget." When she described this episode to me, she wept with incredible sorrow for herself.

She has had two dreams in which she saw interiors similar to that in the original waking dream, but each time with less slush around. When I saw her last week, she said, "I think my heart has more room to breathe ... I don't want to be thin. But I can't seem to hurt myself in the same way." She added, "The great thing is that I did it myself." Then, openly, "I know that isn't altogether true, or is it?" She began to laugh, and so did I.

Pitfalls and Breakthroughs

In the few cases where explorers left treatment before completion, imaginal work was introduced prematurely, or sometimes the translation in action from immaterial to concrete life was prompted too soon. In some instances, the explorers were not sufficiently prepared. Two explorers, for example, (case #6 and 30) came expecting traditional psychotherapy but I introduced them to guided exercises instead. They were both adamant, however, about pursuing a verbal therapy exploring childhood causes of their present problems, and so imaginal work was of no benefit to them. In other instances, patients became frightened by the imaginal existence they encountered and fled from therapy. One explorer (#41) came specifically to do imaginal work. During the guided exercise in initial consultation, she found herself in a meadow where she changed into a tiny insect. Since we had not yet established any sort of rapport at this time, she was too frightened by this experience to return. In hindsight, I should have explored her readiness for imaginal work before actually embarking on guided exercise.

Another example of this is an explorer (case #10) who imaginally encountered a darkening landscape. he was unable to find the sun, and day was merging into night.[12] Throughout his exploration, which verged on hopelessness he experienced intense depression. As with explorer #41, he saw his true state of mind too soon, was overwhelmed and did not return to treatment.

With a phenomenologically based therapy in general, and with waking dream in particular, one begins to find and express one's creative potentials and is freed from the conformist and socially sanctioned habits of familial and societal structure. Waking dream therapy boosts the explorer along in life and helps him surmount a hurdle so that he may begin to move on in his life's direction. For example, a character trait may be modified (as in the case of intimidation); a potential discovered (the eagle soaring); another way of living begun (the alcoholic); an interpersonal difficulty resolved (the young businessman).

Waking dream therapy imparts a new perception about living in the world. Once that new perception has been effected, there is greater freedom available for shaping one's own existence and less dependency on the future as a *thing* one *must* control and manipulate.

Notes

1. For the sake of clarity I want to mention that I intervened in this situation unsolicitedly. I told him not to accept the offer to eat because I was afraid that if he did so, he would become sleepy and then come under the power of these men, be kept a prisoner, and taken out to sea. My subjective ideas impinged on his freedom. This is a very important didactic point for prospective waking dream users.

    In his subsequent report of the waking dream, the patient omitted the part about the invitation. I pointed this out and reminded him of my instructions. He said he *wanted* to eat and was unconcerned about any possible danger.

2. The beginning of this treatment was initiated by a room cleaning exercise, followed by what he described as an unusual dream (see text). A waking dream followed which was based on this dream. His symptoms began to diminish, as described in the text.

3. The concerns with the past, signified by movement to the left, most commonly relates to the mother. In this instance, he looked to his father to save him from spider-mother. Father did not and he remained childishly furious toward father until his work in waking dream.

4. In a particular waking dream a young man (case # 68) is carrying a staff which transforms into a golden ring, which he puts around his neck. The ends don't quite close because of a missing piece which he discovers in his pocket. After putting it in place he takes off the golden ring and rolls it across a green field. He forgot this segment when reporting the waking dream in the next session. Subsequently, a guided exercise was employed where he began by being together with his wife. He put the golden ring around his wife and himself. He went on to report: "my arm is around Joan and we are both looking into the blue sky. The gold ring is around our waists joining us together. I have the eye (given to him by an inner instructor in the waking dream) on my right shoulder. I take the eye and place it in the center of my forehead just above the bridge of the nose. This is my eye of second sight, of inner wisdom. I look at the trees with my third eye and I can see the roots below ground and the sap coursing through them. I look down at the path and I can see underground streams and rocks. I feel wise and powerful, and at peace." He originally came to waking dream therapy in part because of difficulties in interpersonal relatedness. This forgotten segment of the reported waking dream directly alluded to this issue as the guided exercise unfolded. Subsequently his relatedness began to improve noticeably to those around him including his wife.

5. The appearance of red, yellow, and sometimes orange, in night dreams often indicates a physical abnormality, and it may be wise to suggest a physical examination for that person.

6. I use the term *magical* to illustrate the difference between imaginal work and interpretation. The former proceeds from a nonlogical source, while the latter derives from a logical one. As the imaginal event does not happen in the sphere of logical thought it cannot be explained by recourse to logical construction. It was not that the color orange was definitely responsible for the responses of her colleagues, but that it put her in a more receptive, open frame of mind, and so allowed new forms of human engagements to take place.

7. Contingent dependencies are the bases for the causal connections that are perceived to exist between two things, events, or experiences. Contingency is always denoted by the word *because*. In this way nothing is seen to exist of, for or by itself, but exists only because of the presence of some other factor. This factor does not have to be observable; for example, one's present behavior is believed to be caused by past events.

8. One patient (case #100) listed in order, (1)"not to be afraid in work and life," (2)"to complete the doctoral thesis," (3)"to live part of the year near the sea." The treatment was completed in eight months; the order of fulfillment was: (1) no fear, (3) living near the sea, (2) completing the doctoral thesis.

9. During the treatment period explorer #82 wrote much poetry, underwent one guided exercise, four waking dreams, and had many vivid night dreams. Creative works begin to flow from many people undergoing waking dream: books are written, paintings are painted, sculptures wrought, music composed, and poetry written. Explorer #100 went through four guided exercises and two waking dreams, and presented a number of night dreams that changed from black-and-white initially to color.

10. The appearance of a white cape or shawl frequently acts as protection in waking dream.

11. It is quite feasible to bring some aspect of a prior dream experience into waking dream experience if it is required. To bring in an aspect of a lived experience like a dream can enhance waking dream work.

12. When the journeyer finds the setting darkening, a useful way to encourage him to continue his journey is to have him find the sun or wind that will push the clouds away. The sun can often be found by having the patient look up and to the right in the imaginal sky. He will usually see the sun breaking through the darkness and will find the strength and willingness to go on.

Chapter 5

PRINCIPLES FOR UNDERSTANDING

In understanding the principles of phenomenology, there are two points to bear in mind: (1) there is an emphasis on concretizing action in the world (becoming); (2) there is a focus on acausal nondeterminism and its energy component, the movement of will. The movement of becoming requires acting-doing-living, which requires a constant attunement to the present moment. This involves our active effort to read the meaning of signs and to undertake the action necessitated by what the signs point to. This event of choice and effort is will, which initiates action that allows one to create one's existence.

In waking dream therapy, the emphasis is on will and our behavior in relation to this energy. Will concretizes itself as an *intention* to do, find, or learn something. An intention is synonymous with an order, suggestion, and direction (a path to follow). This intention leads us to focus our *attention* on the initiated effort, which serves to set up an *induction* within us to continue on with the effort. As the induction draws us further into the experience, the movement becomes self-sustaining as intention and attention enhance each other (Fig. 5.1).

WILL

↓ ↑

Intention

↓ ↑

Attention

↓ ↑

Induction

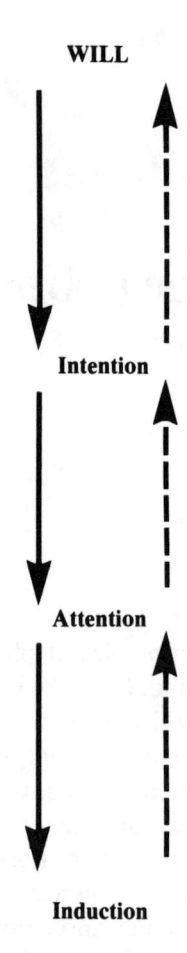

Intention is that which gives direction to the impluse called Will. Intention (or direction) acts to bring Attention to bear on that toward which Will is directed. As Attention is focused, it serves to enhance the action of the senses, thus strengthening and intensifying Induction, or the bringing of the senses to apprehend that toward which Will is directed. This process also works in a reverse manner whereby the action of the senses, Induction, draws Attention which serves to focus Intention, such movement enhancing the impulse of Will.

Figure 5.1

This two-way process describes the waking dream event: we are moved by will to give ourselves an intention, which permits us to focus our attention, thus enhancing the induction, i.e., the drawing of our senses inward through the door by which we enter the imaginal existence. Imagination is at once an *organ of perception* and a *force* that breathes life, or creativity, into the concrete world. Further, if fuels will. Imagination and will act interdependently.

When man discovers the imaginal-spatial realms, he is discovering what is already there. He does not create or project these existences. They constitute a universal experience of man as one of the givens of his existence upon this earth. As man uses his imaginative faculty to explore our holographic universe, he *finds* and *duplicates* what is already there.

The primary laws of this imaginal-spatial dimension are acausal, that is, events are not linked in a sequential fashion, one event determining the next. Therefore, each event is regarded in its own right, speaks for itself, and does not depend on some other event for its existence. This nondeterminism implies a wholeness of perception rather than a fragmentation and dissection of perceptual experience.

Gaston Bachelard has placed imagination in as clear a perspective as anyone who has written on the subject. He notes that imagination is a creative faculty of the mind as distinct from a simple reproduction of perception. Traditionally, imagination is thought of as the faculty of forming images. For Bachelard, however, imagination "is rather the faculty of *deforming* images provided by perception; it is above all the faculty of liberating us from first images here, representations in perception, of *changing* images" (Kaplan, 1972). This freedom from a mental imitation of reality, e.g., sight, Bachelard calls the "function of the unreal." The imaginative force enables man to create new images instead of adjusting to reality as given. Man's capacity to exercise his imagination freely is, for Bachelard, the basic measure of his mental health.

The change and deformation of images result from an

action intrinsic to imagination: "Imagination is the very force of psychic production, more than will or the *élan vital*" (Kaplan, 1972). Imagination is manifested as an aspiration toward new images as well as toward creative fulfillment; it is a liberating force for the human mind.

Understanding the framework of the theories that presently predominate in western psychology is helpful in seeing the points of contact and departure with waking dream and aid in clarifying it as a therapeutic mode. Freud, who, interestingly enough, used a version of waking dream successfully with one patient in 1899 and never used it again (see Chap. 1), elaborated a large structure of theory based on philosophical presuppositions rooted in his commitment to the materialistic-deterministic world view of his time. In many quarters, both within and without psychology, his theory is now taken for fact. Yet as David Bohm, the noted nuclear physicist, recently points out about theory and theorizing in general (1972):

> ... in scientific research, a great deal of our thinking is in terms of *theories*. The word "theory" derives from the Greek "theoria," which has the same root as "theatre," in a word meaning "to view" or "to make a spectacle." Thus, it might be said that a theory is primarily a form of *insight;* i.e., a way of looking at the world, and not a form of *knowledge* of how the world is. [author's emphasis] (p.3)
> ... This means, however, that we do not equate theories with hypothesis. As the Greek root of the word indicates, a hypothesis is a supposition, that is, an idea that is "put under" our reasoning, as a provisional base, which is to be tested experimentally for its truth or falsity. But as is now well known, there can be no conclusive experimental proof of the truth or falsity of a general hypothesis, which aims to cover the whole of reality. Rather, one finds (e.g., as in the case of the Ptolemaic epicycles or of the failure of Newtonian concepts just before the advent of relativity and quantum theory) that older theories become more and more unclear when one tries to use them to obtain insight into new domains. (p.4)
> ... As pointed out earlier, however, this means that our theories are to be regarded primarily as ways of looking at the

world as a whole (i.e., world views) rather than as absolutely true knowledge of how things are (or as a steady approach toward the latter). (p. 5)

A common trap that psychologists fall into is to mistake a way of looking at reality for reality itself. In its adherence to natural science as the *only* scientific approach possible, western science has not avoided this confusion. As an instance of this, consider that current psychology treats, for example, Freud's constructs of ego, id, and superego as realities and vainly attempts to: (1) to prove their existence; (2) to find meaning in mental life by perceiving these theoretical constructs as causes of behavior.

Freud's psychology is "objective." That is, it values what is empirically observable. It assumes that perception leads to thought which is then translated into action. Because of this central pivotal position of thought as the mediator between reality and the individual, Freud relied on reason and intellect as the basis for psychoanalytic method, and on the content of thought for its subject matter. Intellect is the ability to learn and reason, as distinct from the ability to feel and will. Intellect distances itself from experience by speculating, conceptualizing, and theorizing.

Psychology's deterministic tenets can deal only with the effects of rational, sequentially unfolding thought. But, as Ernst Cassirer writes (1944):

> Rational thought, logical and metaphysical thought can comprehend only those objects which are free from contradiction, and which have a consistent nature and truth. It is, however, just this homogeneity which we never find in man. (p. 11)

Phenomenological work values experience itself as the vehicle for becoming. Whereas theory expresses itself as reason, becoming expresses itself in experience. Traditional psychology might approve of the notion of becoming as a suitable goal for therapy, but it still remains wedded to "theories" about emotional life.

For dynamic psychology, "meaning" arises from intellectual interpretation based on linking the past with the present. For phenomenological therapy, "meaning" arises (1) as sign and symbol in the immediacy of the moment, and (2) as pointers to the potentials and possibilities of fulfillment.

When we encounter signs and symbols, we respond to the immediate experience and are not turned toward the past. In brief (see Chap. 6 for a fuller account), symbols can be understood as pointing toward that which is an abstraction, a nonmanifest, non-material expression of the whole. For instance, the Star of David is the symbol of Judaism. Signs, however, are the concrete particulars existing within the whole and usually point to another concrete object. In Judaism, an example of a sign would be the lion, which stands for the tribe of Judah. Signs are embedded within the fabric of the symbol and must be attended to in order to ultimately know the symbol. Signs and symbols are read or understood as telling us about our place in nature and what our actions should be in relation to nature and our fellow man (who are part of that nature as well).

Signs serve four main functions:

1. confirmations
2. corrections
3. pointers toward action to be taken
4. indicators of the law of acausality

As confirmations, signs tell us that some course of action or other that we have embarked on is appropriate. Confirmations usually produce feelings of awe and well-being, or a recognition that something we are doing is correct. A golf ball zooming straight down the fairway is a sign that a golf swing was effective, and we feel gratified.

As a corrective, signs tell us that we have embarked on an incorrect or inappropriate course. Usually there are feelings of displeasure, a recognition of error, and a desire to change. A golf ball slicing off into the woods gives, to many golfers, an unnerving sign of not having performed correctly, and an accompanying feeling of displeasure.

Signs point the way to what needs to be done either to continue the appropriate work or to correct some inappropriate behavior. Regardless of whether action or nonaction is chosen, one is impelled to remain in the present, which is where a sign is *always* located.

To remain in the present is to be attuned to the law of nondeterminism and is to turn away from our habitual attunement to deterministic causality, which is *always* located in the past. Acausality actually embodies the totality of causality, i.e., the four causes: formal, material, efficient, and final, but without giving primacy to the middle two causes. These two are mechanical operations dependent on some initiating effort. Deterministic causality which consists of the middle two causes, cannot account for the variety and creativity of human experience, nor can it explain the essence of man's existence, unless we devaluate man's action to that of a machine.

The acausal principle acts in accordance with final causality, which dictates all of our actions in the world. Final causality is our purpose for existence on this earth. This purpose (some call it God) calls upon us to act, and by so doing, to *become* in order to fulfill our possibilities as a human existence. Every determinist-based therapy rests on final causality in that *all* therapy considers outcome, anticipates cure, or formulates some goal which *dictates* the movement of the therapeutic procedure.

Signs and symbols are, then, related to final cause because they lead man on to the fulfillment of some purpose. They encourage the pursuit of goals or some future occurrence. Deterministic tenets cannot account for formal or final causality or for nondeterminism without destroying the present structure of psychology. If the phenomenological approach infiltrated the present structure of psychology, the field would perhaps develop a more comprehensive vision of human experience.

When we begin to "think" in terms of levels of reality, we are turned toward a new view—one that can have immense implications for psychotherapeutics. We move to a domain where the use of intellect as a vehicle for knowing in human experience is replaced by the fruition of action and the *living of symbols,* as the vehicles for knowing that experience. Waking dream is a phenomenological mode. It consists of action which opens up to knowledge. Our purpose is to fulfill the potentials that the signs and symbols point to.

The foregoing brings us to the second way of understanding "meaning" from the acausal perspective. The images encountered in our experience in both imaginal and everyday life show us what possibilties are available for fulfillment. The translation of these images to their possibilities is the action of giving meaning to them. "Meaning" here represents translation, not interpretation. In imaginal work, one consistently focuses on translation from one framework to another, and not on interpretation i.e., causal explanation. The fulfillment of these possibilities gives life to the form that is our human existence at birth. At birth, we are unfulfilled and have to unfold in our development throughout the course of our lives. These potentials must be concretized throughout our lives. Formal cause is the blueprint of these potentials existing at birth. Of course it also happens that when the potentials are not realized, they often become closed off and inaccessible. As phenomenologists we must disclose these potentials to prospective explorers by pointing out their existence and giving acknowledgment to the genuineness of their existence and permission for their fulfillment.

Freud *believed* that "knowing" one's "unconscious," i.e., intellectually exploring "it" by ferreting out its supposed contents, would provide the key for unlocking the mysteries of the self. "Know thyself" became a prescription to introspect through reason and rational thought processes rather than through the more direct means of experience. Thus, in a deterministic framework reason becomes the mode for reaching liberation. Phenomenologically, the shift is made from knowing via intellect to knowing via experience. As a consequence of this shift the structure of therapy changes.

All therapies that deal with intellectual knowing work within the framework of what can be called the psychology of time. All linear logical thought is a movement in time, and logical language conforms with that movement. This movement governs our functioning as human beings on the level of concrete reality, and so makes possible the social intercourse of human life. But to mistake this causal movement as *the* only principle underlying reality prevents us from achieving in fullness individual freedom and liberation—the avowed goals of all psychological therapeutic endeavors. According to time-bound therapies, i.e., traditional verbal ones, by "knowing" the past we will come to understand our present and so can control our future. This can be done by establishing all of the causal connections between one's history, both private (fantasies, wishes, etc.) and public (relation to family, sex "objects," etc.), and one's present life. But as we have seen, this use of thought is self-deceptive since turning to the past, as linear thought must always do, has to keep us away from the experience of the present moment.

In waking dream, we move from the psychology of time to the *phenomenology of space*. We move outside the linear entropic movement of time as a linear movement (i.e., past→present→future), to the acausal, nondeterministic dimension. In this dimension, linear time is not inherent in its existence. (This is roughly analogous to Freud's idea of the "timeless unconscious.") The movement outside of time permits a recognition of our relationship(s) to life not apprehendable in our everyday habitual, linear, time-oriented life. What occurs outside of time is then brought back to the concrete world and is placed in/directed by linear time. In the experience of waking dream, then, time is *reversed* (as in the night dream) and with it entropy decreases—contrary to what happens in linear time where entropy always increases (Atlan, 1977). Time and entropy, by definition, are always connected.

Linear time is subsumed by space since without the latter,

the former could not exist. The space I refer to, of course, is primary spatiality, qualitatively real and not measurable, within which falls secondary spatiality, or quantifiable, measurable space. The quantifiable time and space coordinates exist in the same dimensions, those of concrete reality.

It is primary spatiality that is implicit in levels of reality or realms of existence. Primary spatiality allows us to be "here" physically while being "there" in reverie, fantasy, or daydream. Our thereness (Heidegger, 1962) is immeasurable and nonquantifiable. If this can be recognized and accepted as a core characteristic of human existence, then our habitual relegation of these experiences to the measurable time dimension in terms of being "unreal" can be overcome. This latter time dimension is quantifiable, linear time measured in seconds, minutes, eons. Any event located in this dimension is assumed to have a "thing" character, i.e., it is quantifiable, measureable, etc. The problem arises in therapeutics when unquantifiable elements such as daydreams and fantasies are seen as "things" that are capable of measurement and of being owned: "I have a fantasy that . . ." So, the contradiction arises in deterministic psychology of owning something that is considered to be "unreal." By understanding the authenticity of *thereness*, these qualitative events achieve a genuineness that is sorely missing in contemporary human experience.

We immediately come upon a fresh insight into the essence of man's experience as total man. Time and space are not equivalent in the phenomenological framework. Rather, time is the stimulus that opens space and permits images to fill it. In order to effect healing of man's emotional suffering the movement of habitual linear time must be stilled momentarily. Such stilling is effected through waking dream. Human existence is a function of time. Time, however, while allowing for an existence in human form, also inhibits knowing our wholeness (healing) and essential unity. Becoming acquainted with the phenomenology of nonmeasurable space, as occurs in waking dream, will permit us to become, hopefully, more comfortable with the phenomenology of space. In space, there can be no psychology simply because one experiences and sees his experience but does not causally think about or causally interpret his experience, i.e., does not commit the experience to the realm of time-bound understanding which is psychology. The experience is returned to the realm of human time by action which places the event in the present concrete reality. To think about or interpret the experience places it in the past, which is the province of psychology. "See" here is meant concretely as in the old rubric, "one picture is worth a thousand words." What is seen, without interpretation or association, is immediately recognized for what it is, and is then immediately known feelingly without question. Understanding this opens up hitherto unexplored possibilities for working with fantasies, daydreams, hallucinations, night dreams, and of course the realm that stands at the core of this book, the imaginal.

The imaginal realm is different from fantasy and daydream. While fantasy and the imaginal state are both different from the waking state, unlike fantasy, the imaginal is simultaneously a state of waking alertness. Joseph Reyher has demonstrated some physiological correlatives of this point in electroencephalographic studies he recorded in the 1960s (Reyher, 1969). The state of human functioning most closely resembling the imaginal is the hypnagogic-hypnopompic, the states of transition between waking and sleeping. Following are some of the major charactersitics that define and distinguish between fantasy and the imaginal realm.

Fantasy

1. Ruminative
2. Time is linear
3. Repetitive and usually unvaried

Imaginal

1. Spontaneous
2. Time is reversed: a nonlinear experience
3. Each experience is unique and fresh

4.	Based on the historical events of the individual's life	4.	Nonhistorical in character, without precedent or antecedent
5.	Compulsive	5.	Autonomous and new, related to what is there at the moment
6.	Wish fulfilling	6.	Wish fulfillment not prominent
7.	Concerned with matter and the concrete world	7.	Takes place in imaginal immaterial realm
8.	Does not lead to creative experience. Based essentially on habitual linear thought processes	8.	Creative and informs concrete world; feelings are varied and can be transmuted into behavior and change
9.	Used for escape from experience	9.	Feel directly part of the experience
10.	Preoccupied, self-involved, self-centered	10.	Loss of sense of self-centeredness and of ordinary space/time dimensions
11.	Not in alert state	11.	Different from waking life but alert state; close to hypnagogic-hypnopompic state
12.	Controlled by the individual	12.	Novel. Always new and not under one's personal control

These distinctions indicate what level the person has reached in waking dream work. Fantasy can be the beginning of imaginal work if it is pushed beyond its habitual frontiers. Attaining the imaginal level bears far different consequences for the personal being and fulfillment from remaining at the fantasy level. The imaginal experience very often gives one a sense of spiritual development and extends fantasy experience to help resolve current emotional imbalances. Such resolution is often necessary before the person can move on to imaginal work. Very often, subjects have to negotiate fantasy lives in initial waking dream work before stepping beyond into the realm of the imagination. Nevertheless, both phenomena, imagination and fantasy, deal with space and existence in space. Understanding this principle does away with having to label and categorize behavior as pathological, psychotic, neurotic, borderline, or whatever. We are concerned with the experience and not with naming a disturbance. Acceptance of experience permits a meaningful exploration of that phenomenon.

To facilitate entering the imaginal realm, there are two fundamental principles to observe. The first is *preparation*. When working in waking dream, the explorer might have to pass through levels of reality within a particular space before reaching the imaginal, that is traversing the habitual fantasy realm may be necessary before he can enter the noetic realm. The instructor must take care not to work at a cross rhythm with the explorer. He must avoid pushing the other too fast. The seeker also might not be ready to explore in this experiential manner right away and might require a period of discussion and building trust before venturing into the imagination.

The second principle basic to entering the imaginal realm, as it is revealed through waking dream is *journeying or making a pilgrimage*. While we are physically *here,* we journey *there.* Consider the implications of this principle for understanding dreams. We are asleep in a bed. As a physical body described as a human being, we are in the bed, yet we are in the domain of the dream setting where all sorts of experiences are occurring. Phenomenologically, we are both *here and there* at the same instant. Physically we are in bed, but essentially we are living our existence in the dream and are closer to those events than to our sense of physically lying in a bed. This capacity to journey to imaginal realms, and learn from the existence directly encountered there makes the experience invaluable because we can bring back this discovery when we return to the realm of concrete reality.

Chapter 6

SYMBOLISM

In waking dream process, symbolism plays a major role, but one that is different from symbolism as it is conventionally understood. In most therapies, a symbol is conceived to be a concrete object which stands for another concrete object. A snake, for example, almost automatically stands for a phallus; or someone unusually concerned with guns or rifles or who dreams about them may be said to be manifesting some concerns about phallic display. It might then be said that the rifle or gun is the symbol of the penis. However, symbols can *only* refer to what is either abstract, immaterial, or unmanifest. One long object, therefore, is not a symbol for another long object. One concrete material thing cannot be a symbol for another concrete material object. One can be a sign for another, when both are of the same class, e.g., both are material forms and exist within the same system, that is, *long* objects. But to discuss both of these concrete forms as representing power, maleness, or strength is a correct use of the symbolic mode.

Misperceiving a sign for a symbol elevates that sign to a

more magisterial position over and above the other signs. It is like saying that the statue of Baal has greater significance than any other stone statue. When a concrete form is apprehended in this way, then idol worship becomes the fate and degradation of the symbol. Since psychology has failed to make this crucial distinction between sign and symbol, this discipline is unable to accommodate a transcendent quality in man's existence and cannot, therefore, incorporate this most vital quality into psychotherapy. Without this understanding of the symbolic mode, transcendent events become reduced to *material forms* dynamically stated as: "fantasies of merging symbiotically with the all-giving, all-powerful mother in a regressive reunion where one was once an omnipotent infant."

Symbols do not result from assigning one concrete or material object to stand in place of another. When two objects exist on the same level, one stands as a sign for the other. Strictly speaking, this sort of concrete object for concrete object substitution should be called semiotics, or the study of signs. In waking dream, however, the emphasis moves past the signified object to the knowledge that the symbol represents. We separate the signifier from the signified[1] and see that we as human beings are the signifiers of the signified lying beyond our physical presence; we see that the personal "I" does not produce the universe.

When a concrete object points the way to something transcendent, ineffable, not subject to description by the ordinary use of language, then we are dealing with symbol; and symbols link us to that which is not accessible to us by the ordinary use to which we put our senses.

The tree is a felicitous example that can be used to demonstrate the concrete manifestation of the possibility of transcendence. Transcendence is a possibility accorded to us as humans by virtue of our being born as humans. The tree's existence shows us how to attain such freedom and liberation. The roots are planted firmly in the earth. The trunk grows straight, strong, and sturdy. The branches and its leaves grow up and out toward the sky. A human being must grow in the same way. He must plant his feet firmly on the ground, and then he can grow straight and cultivate his possibilities. As he faces his possibilities and fulfills these potentials, he grows more and more free. The seed[2] becomes fulfilled only by manifesting forth through a process of doing or living. This becoming is the unfolding of our development.

Another important distinction about symbols that arises out of waking dream exploration is that we do not create symbols as is so commonly assumed by western psychological writers. On the contrary, we receive and apperceive the symbolic realm which encases us at every instant. We do not create symbols, we are symbols, live in symbols, and penetrate symbols. They are present all the time and can be observed by us every day in the world around us by an action of will. The act of taking a step can be seen as a symbolic gesture, initiated by an act of will. We could not walk unless we knew that walking is possible within space. There can be no movement without space. To move implies the knowledge of primary spatiality existing "out there." Thus we know we are the symbol—the bridge between *there* and *here*.

The readers of this book are most probably aware of the vast literature describing the meaning, nature, construction, formation, development, and understanding of symbols and symbolism. It does not seem, judging by the literature, that one can capture the core of this elusive subject. We know that symbols are links between the revealed and the unrevealed.[3] They possess *necessity* by dint of being links which forever urge us toward unity, to counterbalance our living in a world divided and fragmented by our interpretations and our insistence that we are only separate individual objects defined by a specific location in space that is measurable and quantifiable.

For psychotherapists, a central issue has been how to use the supposed "symbol-making process" of the patient. Different psychologic therapies conceive of and use symbols differently, usually depending upon the importance of the "unconscious" in the schema. Behavior modification, for example, which has no interest in unconscious conflict or motivation, pays no heed to symbols. In traditional dynamic therapy, symbols are moderately important, whereas in Jungian therapy, they are preeminently important. However, all of the current systems that use symbolism have one thing in common: they stress that the understanding of symbols leads to insight, which has value in effecting some sort of healing.

As a phenomenological form, waking dream does not emphasize the use of reason as the primary way to knowing. It stresses the fulfillment of being through the function of *living* as an actional event. So instead of understanding the symbol through interpretation, *one lives the function of the symbol* (or at least makes the attempt). This is accomplished by penetrating the symbol—symbol being that directly apprehendable concretization of what is more hidden, unrevealed, and *nonconcrete: in short, symbol is image.*

It is my contention that the knowing of our human existence comes about through the action of living the function of the symbol in one's imaginal existence and then translating that knowledge into action in everyday life. Symbol, as bridging function, allows a coming and going from material to nonmaterial reality, and back again. In this way we fulfill our being. Knowing as a function of reason and logical deduction often stands as a barrier to action and thus stands in the way of wisdom. Thinking allows us to "obtain" only partial, fragmented, analytical knowledge, never wisdom which is whole and synthesized. Unfortunately, we often mistake that partial knowledge for the whole truth.

We feel the urge to come back together again, to unify. But how? By living the symbol! Penetrate the symbol and experience your oneness with it. Become unified with the symbol and learn that you are linked with what appears to be divided. To interpret the symbol can bring only a partial awareness of the fundamental unity of our existence, which can then be fully realized by entering into it via the imaginal experience. Once experienced, there is no longer any need to interpret. An instance of living the symbol is the effort of active contemplation where one attempts, in a clear state of mind, to concentrate attention on a symbol as in many systems of meditation.

Fulfillment occurs through doing. We are born and therefore come into existence, although with ignorance. We possess all the possibilities of our being but are as yet ignorant of their fulfillment. We then come to know these possibilities through action. This action is always freely undertaken with full command out of an awareness of choice. There is inhibition of action but one is always aware of that. There is no "unconscious" motivation preventing action; rather, there have been proscriptions against engaging in action as a consequence of faulty social conditioning. We turn away from fulfillment. We are not unaware of what is turned away from, nor are we unaware or "unconscious" of the fear attendant on facing what calls to us from "out there"; but we lack the will to take action and instead rationalize away our insufficiencies.

Once action occurs we have immersed ourselves in the fabric of life and have become part of life. It is this continuous act of becoming through action that results in the fulfillment of potentials. This fulfillment *is* the actualization of our being that brings with it whole knowledge. It is this knowledge of becoming that constitutes the essential fulfillment of human existence. It is the recapturing through action of our essential unity with the movement of life. As this becoming takes place, we, step by step, lose the sense of our personal "I" (or ego), which up to this point had been thrust to the center of experience as the "I" who knows this, the "I" who thinks that, etc., that has effected the split into subject and object. This fundamentally dualistic view of life constitutes the original stage of being with ignorance where the personal "I" predominates.

The paradox is that at the same time we live the symbol, we ourselves *are* the symbol. Our physical existence called human being points the way to that which is hidden and not material. In trying to understand what symbols do, it might be said that they serve to permit us to recognize at once the existence of this paradox as an essential mode of our living in the world as well as showing the way toward resolution of the paradox. An object can only be considered a symbol if it demonstrates this paradoxical quality. In this regard, man can be said to be a symbol—a symbol of the movement of the ineffable bearing its unity and diversity at the same time. The material and nonmaterial inheres in the symbol at the same time. The sensory world of concrete reality can also be said to be symbolic of that which stands beyond human existence and is not ordinarily apprehendable by the senses. Both man and the world are their own paradoxes existing in relation to ordinary sensory awareness and yet always pointing to that which lies behind ordinary sensory awareness: man and the world existing in/as a different reality. Symbols, in effect, are the language of the other levels of reality.

It can be recognized that the world as it exists in the immediacy of our perception *is* the symbol for God. As inhabitants of this world, human beings are part of that great symbol since we are formed in "God's image." We are the concretization of that fundamental truth. But our way to God is mediated by other levels of reality. While these other levels do not body forth in concrete form, they do inform and mediate physical human existence. We are not symbol-making organisms as traditional psychology would have it, but instead we are the concrete symbol of an energy, of which our brain is the mediator.

Symbolic exploration in waking dream occurs along three distinct lines: (1) what symbols do, (2) what a symbol is from the phenomenological-spatial perspective, and (3) how symbols are used when working in spatiality.

A symbol is both a clue and an expression of the existence of the nonmanifest. Symbols themselves are reminders, pointers toward the nonmaterial levels that inform our existence.

The "how" of symbols refers to the living of their function. We live the function by imagining the experience of the developmental phases of a created form, say a tree, by apprehending the nature of that created form, which involves birth, transformation, and death.

The paradox that must be embraced here is that at the moment of our birth, we announce our dying. The full bloom of the rose is the culmination of its gestation and at the same time the announcement of its proximate death. All the green we see about us in nature represents the death process of that nature. Similarly, all the growth we attain and aspire to inevitably leads us to the fulfillment of that end, the fulfillment of being —death to the world of time and limitations. The fundamental error made by traditional psychology is to view this growth process as a "regression," to a "return to the womb" or backward pull, since growth by definition implies a push forward or up. But to fulfill being properly, we must live, and live to the utmost of our possibilities.

Life is a two-stage process. The first stage is the nine months of preparation during which we as human beings must lie quiescently and develop all the equipment we are going to need. Then at the moment when all is ready, we burst forth into the world. The leap from the eternal environment of the womb releases both living and dying at the same instant. We are forever moving forward to reach from wherever it is we emanated. In this way our movement through life is both circular and linear.[4] We are impelled to move forward just as our physical development pushes relentlessly and automatically to its limits. The physical push forward depends on the dying of cells. When the cells of our body cease to die, we die physically.

In waking dream work, explorers commonly go through preparatory, gestational, birthlike experiences. Explorers quite often find themselves in long dark passageways or tunnels that they compare to a birth canal. One person even likened the consistency of the walls of the passageway to the walls of the female reproductive system. Characteristically, they will find a light at the end of the passageway. The emergence into this light is often experienced as a powerful crescendo, or a sudden abrupt plunge. The light is often experienced as blinding or exceptionally bright. The explorers often comment, "I feel like I have been reborn."

When considering symbols within the framework of a phenomenology of being, we are not dealing with the interpretation or knowing of symbols through an intellectual process, but rather through a process of linking ourselves to the ordinarily inaccessible knowledge of a different self. This knowledge becomes available only through living the function of the symbol, thus making concrete what is fundamentally immaterial via this action.[5]

This understanding of symbolism is rewarding for both therapist and patient. The therapist can escape from a reductionistic and preconceived bias about his relationship to the world. Neither interpreting nor confining oneself to the material meaning of a symbol brings with it the habit of keeping an open mind. The patient, through regarding symbols as I have suggested, can expand his possibilities for fulfillment by coming in touch with a different level of his existence, and often can recognize an escape from his habitual tendencies and patterns.

Simply put, symbol is the link or the bridge among the several spatial existences in which a human entity can live. It allows us to move between the material and nonmaterial worlds and thus gives us information about the nature of nonmaterial reality. It is essentially an extrarational means of transmitting that knowledge. By extrarational, I mean that the bridging or linking function of symbols cannot be gleaned by the use of rational intellect.

As an example of penetrating the symbol, the artist (case #90) described earlier entered the following waking dream after a night dream in which she was standing on the balcony at the top of an orange-domed temple.

> I am standing on the top balcony of my temple. The dome changes from being three feet high to become enormous, making me a tiny figure beside it. Then it becomes smaller again and I enter through a plain rectangular door. I want to leave the door

open for light; I reject an offer of a lantern or flashlight [my suggestion].
A glow of light comes up from the bottom. I float around in the inside of the egg-shaped space. The top part is open and clear. Below the middle line is a jellylike substance, greyish in color around the edges. But it parts to make a passageway for me. As I descend further down the substance becomes netlike, a tan-yellowish color. It continues to part as I descend. There is a gold ladder attached to the side walls of the egg which curve in towards the bottom.
At the bottom I expected to see pools of blue water but instead I see a tiny pin-prick hole of very intense white light coming through. I think that I should be able to go through this opening, but I cannot. So I decide to look through it. It is about chest-waist level so I have to kneel down to put my eye to the hole, but when I do it disappears. I back up and see it again. I walk toward it cautiously but as I come within three feet, it disappears again.
I am feeling very disappointed when I realize that the light wants to come to me. I stand still and it moves up and enters my body. I feel filled out to the edges of my skin with this marvellous, throbbing white light. I expand inside. I see waves on the ocean and become one with them. The throbbing light inside me joins the back and forth motion of the waves. I lose all sense of my body and I become a gentle pulsating rhythm and transparent light. It is wondrous.
With some reluctance I go back up the ladder stairs to the top part of the egg and exit onto the balcony of the temple. I step off onto the ground and see the tree from my first waking dream. Beside it is the red flower smiling, almost teasing me. I pick the flower and stick it behind my ear. It grows into a petal cap which covers my head and cascades down my shoulders and back.

In her subsequent discussion of this event, she felt that she had been striving too hard after her artistic expression. She thought now of approaching her work more meditatively, more in the spirit of Zen. She would become more receptive and allow the creative energy to come to her and fill her. She would join that flow.

The role of symbolism in imaginal work has another important dimension. I refer to the importance of considering the meaning of the movement in space—especially the overall principle of ascension and descent—from another perspective. One of the significant contributions the waking dream makes to therapeutics is to bring to awareness the meaningfulness of the vertical axis; whereas the common therapeutic emphasis up to now has been on working within the horizontal axis. Let me expand on this.

There are two ways of looking at reality. According to Mircea Eliade:

> The chief difference between the man of the archaic and traditional societies and the man of modern societies with their strong imprint of Judaeo-Christianity lies in the fact that the former feels himself indissolubly connected with the Cosmos and cosmic rhythms, whereas the latter insists that he is connected only with history. (1954, p. xiii–xiv)

The two perspectives can be visualized as horizontal and vertical. Our daily life takes place on the horizontal axis or plane. On this plane, reality occurs in historical time in a world of measurable height, width, and depth. Imaginal life takes place on the vertical axis or plane, which is ahistorical and imbued with the divine, or that which is eternally recurrent. Signs are a movement of horizontality, whereas symbols are a movement of verticality. Signs are contiguous to each other and operate within a linear mode. An example would be the drawing or cardboard figure of a man on the washroom door in a restaurant. Symbols point to that which is not tangible, not immediately apprehendable, not contiguous, and to something higher in our nature.

The language describing levels of consciousness—"ascending to the heights," "plumbing the depths," "the depths of the unconscious," "heaven above," "hell below"—attests to an intuitive recognition of verticality. Here the movement is up and down and we can reach heights and depths impossible to attain when journeying in the horizontal realm of predictable, ordered dimensions. Waking dream allows the self to be in touch with lofty feelings and dark ones; open feelings or buried ones. The characteristic posture of the explorer in waking dream is, therefore, upright, placing him in a physical position of verticality.

The vertical axis is recognized transculturally. The Old Testament describes Jacob's dream: "and behold a ladder was set up on the earth, and the top of it reached to heaven: and behold the angels of God ascending and descending on it." Jacob's dream is no ordinary dream. Few dreams of either patients or non-patients are about angels. Just as the angels in Jacob's dream stand between man and God, so does the imaginal realm stand between the concrete reality and the level of highest abstract reality.

The vertical axis is prominent in the great Chinese book, *I Ching* or *Book of Changes* (Baynes & Wilhelm, 1950), which tells us that humans stand between heaven and earth and are vehicles for the interplay of forces between heaven and earth. *I Ching* reveals its knowledge in the form of hexagrams or six-lined vertical figures composed of two three-lined trigrams. The top line of each trigram stands for heaven, the middle for humans, the bottom for earth. Human beings integrate heaven (spirit) and earth (matter). The same representation of the harmonization of matter and spirit is found in the Christian symbol of the cross, where vertical (spirituality) and horizontal (matter) axes cross and proclaim the totality of human beings. In all cultures, the realm of spirit is symbolized by a central axis, which is often represented by the tree of life, pyramids, or a ladder. The central axis is always vertical and always alludes to the spiritual.

Verticality has always meant breaking out of the confines that bind us or inhibit our movement toward freedom, liberation, and transcendence (Eliade 1975b, p. 110,118). It allows communication between the levels of being. Verticality is always linked to ascension (and automatically thereby to descent) and to flight. Here flight means movement into spatial dimensions or the journey(s) of waking dream. By enacting such journeys, we become aware of our *thereness,* that which transcends the limits imposed by our engaging in the physical dimension of existence, which for convenience can be termed our *hereness.*

In hereness, quantity, and "things" become the overwhelming priority in life. Since "things" are by nature static and have defined limits, we lose the experience of flow, change, and movement which address themselves to the qualitative side of life. We do not see that what is realized in the imaginal existence can sanctify our material life. Generally, we do not take the opportunity to travel vertically because we are habituated to living in a mechanized, material existence.

Moving on the vertical axis means either ascending or descending. Each movement has its own evocative potential. Ascending usually helps a person break out of a situation that has become blocked. It allows a person to change a situation, to find the way to overcome the habitual tendencies that chain him to a constricted and limited existence.

In a waking dream, one woman (case #135) entered a door using a key shaped like a cross. She found herself in a vast room with marble floors and vaulted arches made of glass that extended skyward. Light was streaming in, and she heard the sound of a church choir singing. She could not see the choir but she listened attentively. As she did so, she found herself floating up. She said, "It is as though my spirit has been liberated." She rose on a beam of light that was streaming through the glass arch, feeling that she was joining the sounds she was hearing.

In waking life, this woman began to notice that she always surrendered her own perceptions to the opinions of others. She also noticed that when she did this, she experienced a tightness in her chest and abdomen. Subsequent to her imaginal work, she became more assertive and committed to her own ideas and perceptions rather than to others' ideas and perceptions, which had been the case previously. For example, she attended a talk given by a professional person for whom she had considerable respect. She had always accepted his statements about life uncritically and rather compliantly. At this talk, she found she did not agree with what he was saying, and felt that his comments were unclear; and further that she did not understand what he was talking about. Her prior participation in the symbolic realm via waking dream allowed her to participate more fully and independently in the sign realm through the vehicle of a professional talk she attended.

While ascending helps the person move transcendently, descending helps him plumb his own depths. Desoille's original motifs were chosen to help the patients explore their personal and interpersonal life, and many of them involve descent. When exploring imaginally, the patient usually finds the direction that has direct bearing on his problems, and often he must descend before he can find ascent useful. Once the descent is made the explorer is asked to ascend, bringing with him whatever he has discovered before terminating the journey.

In ordinary therapeutic work, the issues primarily encountered are the patient's self-preoccupation and repetitive patterns, which are usually non-creative. These patients tend to find the downward path more helpful at first because that direction is tantamount to a descent into the center of oneself which must first be lived before the movement to freedom, denoted by ascent, can be accomplished.

One explorer (case #42), mentioned earlier, began to climb a mountain that had appeared in a dream. As he climbed, he became more frightened. The foliage became sparser and sparser as he went on. As the surroundings "disappeared," he became increasingly more afraid. It was only on the descent that his fear diminished. As he descended he met a frightening creature who advanced towards him, but he stood his ground and the creature went right by him, permitting him to continue his descent.

The ascent seems to be a call reminding the person of his possibility for fulfilling the immaterial component of life to which as yet he has not attended. The ascent is an *action* of *thereness*. Here, we can ascend physically, as in climbing stairs, climbing mountains, and boarding rockets. This ability to enact potentials is even more meaningful when we consider that *through action, we can reconcile the transcendent and the commonplace in our lives.*

Ascent is often revelatory. This experience is frequently depicted in mythology, epics, and other forms of literature. Just one example is that of the Old Testament prophets: the epiphanies of Moses, Isaiah, and Elijah occurred on mountain tops. In our daily lives, we have the same possibility of transcending the limits imposed by quantitative life. *But we ascend not in order to escape from life, but in order to enrich life as it is lived on the plane of physical existence.* Through ascent, we see that we are the agents for concretizing the abstract, nonmanifest, or divine on earth, and that at the same time we are the agents for extracting the abstract, nonmanifest, and divine on earth out of the occurrences of ordinary, daily experience.

This realization makes it possible to work toward overcoming excessive self-involvement and acquisitiveness. It is part of our dependency on external form, be it another person or an object, such as money, to validate our existence. The irony of our existence is that what we depend on in fact is not dependable, but unpredictable and uncontrollable because it is external to us. Thus we are devastated when the external form fulfills its own nature, contrary to our expectations and needs, and we suffer its unavailability, or what is even worse, its loss.

The encounter with the vertical axis alters man's perceptions about his relationship to the world. In part, the discovery of new realms of experience helps us realize that concrete reality is part of an overall hierarchy of realities. This leads to a recognition of connection with a greater whole, of which the physical existence in the world of concrete reality is only a part, and with this recognition comes humility. Narcissism must retreat in the face of humility.

At the same time, we experience a freedom that allows us to see the limiting nature of our narcissistic disposition. Once we experience this freedom, we realize that what we have been desperately clinging to—fame, money, power, other people—as "things" to possess in order to enhance our self-esteem or sense of personal "I"-ness, is really unnecessary. In narcissism, the child in the man rules the adult in the man. The action of ascent helps us to put the child in his place.

Descent along the vertical axis permits exploration of the center, as it were, of the personal existence. All men want to know their origins. This desire takes forms as diverse as anthropology, archaeology, and exploration. Its expression in psychology is the psychologist's wanting to know the origin of illness or conflict.

Ancient man sought the same knowledge as contemporary man. For all men, the vertical axis grows out of the center, which is the zone of absolute reality where all creation takes place. To attain the center—through ritual or the "conscious repetition of given paradigmatic gestures" (Eliade, 1954, p. 5) —is to grasp the essential reality of the world. In symbolic language, the center is often referred to as the "navel of the world." This "navel" is a vertical axis, or *axis mundi*, which is the meeting point of heaven, earth, and underworld, the three cosmic zones. To be complete, human existence, then or today, must take into account not only the sensory, material, objective world, but also the immaterial, sensory reality of the nonobjective world.

Mircea Eliade has written about the vertical axis:

> ... now, the type of "waking dream" that Desoille most frequently requires of his patients is precisely that of ascending a staircase or climbing a mountain. To put it another way, he obtains psychic cures by reanimating in active imagination, certain symbols which comprise, in their own structure, the ideas of "passage" and of "ontological mutation." In the frame of reference in which they were known to the historian of religions, these symbols express the *attitudes* taken up by man and at the same time, the *realities* he is confronting, and these are always sacred realities, for, at the archaic level of culture, the *sacred* is the pre-eminently *real.* Thus, one may say, the simple repetition, aided by an active imagination, of certain symbols which are

religious (or which, more exactly, are abundantly attested in innumeral religions), brings about a psychological improvement and leads ultimately to a recovery.... Gaston Bachelard has justly defined the technique of the waking dream as a form of the *imagination of movement.* [author's emphasis] (Eliade, 1975b, p. 117–118).

This "movement," which is so characteristic of imaginal work, puts one in touch with experience that is not apprehendable by logic. The movement of verticality operates in the nonrational sphere of thought and is not subject to the laws of logic. The sacred, or religious experience, therefore, must be known by a process not available to psychology. Psychology deals with what is rational and intellective and subject to analysis. Movement relates to what is synthesized and made into wholeness.

This is where imagination fits into the scheme of fashioning an approach towards mitigating emotional disturbance. To date, no single western therapeutic approach—Freudian, Jungian, and the like—harmonizes or strives toward the unity of matter and spirit. The germ of such an approach resides in psychoanalytic treatment, and such integrative attainment is often achieved largely in the phenomenological-analytic method of Medard Boss, the Swiss psychoanalyst (1963, 1979), and Hubert Benoit, the French psychoanalyst (1959, 1973). However, as much as it seems to me that Boss's work extends psychoanalysis to its furthest and most fruitful limits, western psychotherapeutic processes still omit the contribution of the imaginal life, necessary for a balance of the lexical and verbal. The Jungian analysts use a form of imagery work in which they set about interpreting the imaginal events along mythological and archetypal lines, thereby translating the events to an analytic, logical framework.

Uninterpreted, standing on its own, imagination allows us to cut through the veil of material life and allows us to fulfill our real task—the aim of all psychotherapeutic treatment—that of attaining freedom and liberation in their truest sense. Imagination may be viewed from this perspective as the central faculty acting as a vital bridge between sense and intellect, mind and body, spirit and matter.[6]

Since traditional psychology has chosen not to encompass the experiences of the vertical axis, it has been unable to incorporate the spiritual impulse into its body of knowledge. Unfortunately, this insufficiency has been replaced by a dogmatic denial of the genuineness of religious and spiritual phenomena. It is quite clear that a materialistically based system cannot address itself to what is a nonmaterial event (although that nonmateriality may be physiologically recorded at some level).

It commonly happens that explorers involved in extensive imagery work spontaneously discover the religious or spiritual potential even though they might have previously abjured such a possibility in the course of ordinary conversation.[7]

One patient (case #51), a man in his late 20s, had no ostensible tie to any religious tradition and came from a family of mixed religious denominations that now espoused atheism. His waking dream therapy lasted one year. During this time he experienced a waking dream in which he was flying over the desert. He landed and discovered that it was the Sinai. There, he discovered three figures coming toward him: a large one accompanied by two smaller ones who appeared to be young boys. The central figure turned out to be Moses, who was to be the patient's instructor. He was quite surprised that such an eminent religious figure would play so significant a role in his life.

In a later discussion about Moses, he said that he was put in touch with his Judaism and, more specifically, his link with God. Moses was as close to a direct contact with God as he could conceive. Before his therapy concluded, he was to take several journeys with Moses, who helped him to discover dimensions of unselfishness and caring for others (which is a frequent experience within verticality). This coming out of oneself and recognizing the importance of the other is an integral part of the religious and spiritual experience.

At every level of culture, regardless of differing historical contexts, the symbolism of ascent invariably expresses the abolition of the limited human condition (i.e., suffering and pain), and promotes transcendence, and freedom (Eliade, 1969).

The vertical plane makes freedom of movement possible between one mode of existence and another. As Eliade points out in several places (1969,1975b), this freedom of movement allows one to change a situation and in so doing, to abolish a conditioning system or, in other terms, to change a habit. Regeneration occurs: "yesterday's profane and illusory existence gives place to a new, to a life that is real, enduring, and effective." (1954, p. 18)

In the experience of ascent, time is overcome and the ascender is catapulted into the *presence of the present,* that eternal moment where he becomes contemporary with the moment of creation. Here in the *presence of the present,* the individual's history, possibilities, and purpose are summarized. One cannot remain in this moment, just as one cannot remain in the womb forever, but he is thrown into the world of time and space, where what has been gleaned must be put into action by the counterpart of imagination—will. Will initiates action whereby change is effected in the concrete world.

Waking dream process brings about a new use of the senses, which is to explore the imaginal rather than the concrete; and it brings about a change in our axial relationship to the world, from horizontal to vertical. We move beyond historical time and measureable space. Waking dream exploration makes these movements possible by allowing the voyager to penetrate spatiality, otherwise apprehended as image, and condensed as symbol.

NOTES

1. In the instance of the snake and the phallus, both are signifiers of that which they signify, the concept.

2. Just as the tree is the articulation of the seed (its essent or virtuality), so man is the articulation of his seed as he blossoms forth on the path of becoming (Schwaller de Lubicz, 1977). As this occurs he fulfills the essence of his being.

3. Strictly speaking, a symbol can only be a symbol if it makes direct reference to the connection between man and those other levels, and ultimately to God. It is of interest with regard to the latter that the first meaning given to "symbol" in the Oxford English Dictionary is that pertaining to the authoritative beliefs of the Christian church.

4. This is the movement of the spiral, perhaps the most fundamental movement in nature.

5. This movement toward union with levels of reality other than the concrete world is akin to the aim of primitive ritual. "Man of a traditional culture sees himself as real only to the extent that he ceases to be himself (for a modern observer)" and escapes profane time by returning to "the mythical time of the beginning of things," *in illo tempore, ab origine.* He achieves this "abolition of time through the imitation of archetypes and the repetition of paradigmatic gestures. . . . revealed by a god *ab origine,* . . . in other words, every sacrifice repeats the initial sacrifice and coincides with it." (Eliade, 1954, pp. 34–35, ix) Thus he reunites himself with the zone of absolute reality and loses the sense of himself as an individual personality.

Eliade notes that "of all the vital sciences, only psychoanalysis arrives at the idea that the 'beginnings' of every human being are blissful and constitute a sort of Paradise, whereas the other vital sciences stress especially the precariousness and imperfection of the beginnings." (1975a, p. 89). That is, ritual and psychoanalysis and waking dream all seek the same goal—liberation—but with different techniques and from different viewpoints.

6. Henry Corbin has illustrated this point in many ways. For a fuller discussion see his: *Creative Imagination in the Sufism of Ibn'Arabi,* and *Spiritual Body and Celestial Earth,* both published by Bollingen Foundation vol. XCI parts 1 and 2. Princeton: Princeton Univ. Press 1969 and 1977 respectively.

7. The reader may object that my own interest in this dimension might color the patient's experience. I can only say that I do not interfere with what the patient experiences, nor do I attempt to direct what is discovered. To do so would violate one of the cardinal working principles of waking dream therapy, i.e., finding it/finding out for oneself. One must be open to the discovery of *any* possibility and meet it in an accepting manner.

Chapter 7

THE THERAPEUTIC RELATIONSHIP

What is the nature of the therapeutic relationship in waking dream therapy? Does it differ from the traditional relationship in verbal therapy?

In phenomenological approaches, the therapeutic role can be divided into two aspects: as instructor and as advisor to the explorer. The instructor directs the explorer through the world of imaginal reality; the advisor supports the patient's attempts to enact his will through experience in the everyday life of concrete reality. The explorer has previously not been granted permission to carry out those imperatives that are the task of each of us. He is afraid, he ventures forth; he is tentative and somewhat unsure; he turns to the advisor for assurance, permission and care so that he may continue. Besides providing nurture, the advisor helps the explorer to see which potentials are available for fulfillment and which are closed to him so that energy can be meaningfully directed. The advisor encourages the actualization of possibilities while recognizing that what is "present to fulfill' is synonymous with potential.

By encouraging and helping the explorer to find potentials, the advisor explicitly conveys that there is *hope*. This hope is concretely translated to mean that there are options open for a freer existence in which we concomitantly come to recognize that we are not enslaved, nor consigned to repetitive behaviors. But *the individual must find this out for himself.* The advisor may indicate that potentials exist and he may promote living them through, but he has to refrain as much as possible from indicating that these potentials must be fulfilled or from prematurely pushing the searcher—who will pursue the potentials when he is ready. The searcher must remember, however, that once the potential is discovered, it must be realized, that is, concretized.

The instructor/advisor points out that reality is not what it appears to be and that the world of things does not constitute the only reality of a human existence. He further apprises the explorer that the apprehension of reality occurs through experience or action taken without previous prejudices about what is possible and not possible. The instructor/advisor does not, under any circumstance, undertake or usurp the explorer's experience. The explorer is always left free to find what he has to find in order to fulfill himself. The explorer may call upon the instructor/advisor for some assistance if he meets an obstacle or for some answer to a question that inhibits his action or his finding. *From the outset* the instructor/advisor has given permission to the explorer to abandon all preconceived notions about what is real and unreal. In addition, the instructor/advisor has opened or cleared a space in which the explorer can venture forth to find what reality is for himself. The explorer is not limited to searching only in the *here* of his existence but can also explore the *there*.

The therapist–patient relationship as it is constructed in the psychology of *here* limits itself to recognizing the problems that are bounded by measurable space and time. In a sense, problems *are* bounded in this way: one must be freed from maladaptive behavior in the concrete world. But this is only the beginning, the preparation for what is *necessarily* the next step —the journey to *there,* or penetrating the noetic by means of waking dream. Not only should patients regard this work as preliminary to the more arduous task of finding the *totality of existence,* but also those calling themselves "therapists" should be equally cognizant and as searching as those whom they are attempting to treat. A well-grounded therapy should address itself to concrete and imaginal realities.

Without an appreciation of the instructor-explorer relationship *that has to obtain in full and healing therapeutic work,* one may not help to produce any significant transformation in an individual's existence. Those psychologists who limit reality to *here* and thus assume that concrete life can answer all the questions of our existence, are indulging in "magical" thinking. They believe in the unobservable cause leading indubitably to an observable effect. Here is a common example: "I am crying *because* you yelled at me" is generally accepted as a "truth." But the only facts are the acts of crying and yelling. The reconstructed cause can only be presumed to exist. To cry is but one of a myriad responses to what is encountered. My response, in any circumstance, *is my response* and is *not predicated or contingent* on what I encounter and that which might be called the cause of that response. If I persist in believing that your yelling made me cry, then I give up my freedom to exist autonomously and I continue to repudiate my responsibility for my responses. Yelling is not an inherent part of crying and doesn't necessarily belong to crying. Consonant with the habit of dependent-contingent thinking, conventional therapy seeks explanations for habitual crying that is now past. The assumption is that once the causal relationship between emotional responses is explained, its effects will not recur under those or similar circumstances. To "explain", the therapist accounts for all the steps that supposedly occurred between the yelling and the crying, since he assumes that one has caused the other. He may relate the parents' repetitive yelling at the child to the adult's crying now, even though the parents' yelling is not now present. But it is not why you cry that is important but *that* you cry instead of choosing any other possible action. Guilt is compounded when the one who yells is told that his action *makes* another cry. Then he is made to feel guilty for his behavior as well as for the other's crying. But one's responsibility for the action of the other is questionable. If I am responsible for your behavior, then I am just as helplessly tied to you as you are to me. We both are not free, although I have the sneaking suspicion that if we each took the appropriate responsibility for our own action, i.e., stopped the habit of blaming others, and seeing contingencies, we would both recognize that we are *free from the outset.*

It is then by the paradoxical action of leaping out of one magical world, that inhabited and constructed by linear thought (at once illusory but also paradoxically concretely real) to another magical world, that of nonlinear, nonrational, imaginal thought, that we can move to complete our existence as fully as possible. We move from the habitual magical world of linear thought to the free magical world of imagination and return to the former ready to try and live this existence with less habitual rationality. That is to say, we try to live by doing, not by substituting rational thinking for living. Rational thinking provides a preparatory stage for living, but in our psychologizing culture it has become synonymous with living.

The essence of the relationship of instructor to explorer is an *attitude of open acceptance* of all that is encountered in this world and in oneself and the other as genuine and authentic. In such an environment, the explorer can also develop an acceptance of himself, which is essential to bringing about change and transformation. In my experience, the therapeutic attitude of open acceptance is what leads to healing, and those therapies which operate without this acceptance do not produce significant change in an individual's patterned existence.

The phenomenologist perceives the meeting of the two participants as being without precedent. In phenomenologically based therapy, the therapist is who he is from the outset and is not to be mistaken for anyone else in the patient's life. Similarly, the patient is a real person not misperceived by the therapist as anyone else in his life. That the patient strives to preserve the distinction becomes one focus of the therapeutic endeavor.

As one example of this, let us consider the current notion of "transference." From the phenomenological position, "transference" is the perceptual distortion that leads the person to habitually perceive the present and past as identical and to respond to them as if they were identical. It is not important to the phenomenologist that perceptual distortion is directed at someone, but rather, the *fact* that the perceptual distortion occurs.

The working principle of waking dream therapy, as for all phenomenological techniques, is to say "yes" to human experience and to embrace each individual's way of being in the world. (Embracing is not to be confused with condoning. Embracing accepts behavior, feeling, or thinking as genuine, but condoning gives license to actions that may impede the freedom of another to exist in the world and is a different matter.) This immediate acceptance of the other's authenticity contravenes the tendency of current psychology and psychiatry, which habitually categorize and dichotomize the patient's behavior, feeling, and thinking as pathologic or normal. What is built into this way of perception is a negatively judgmental and essentially nonaccepting relationship to what is encountered in the world. On the other hand, by accepting the phenomenon as is, the therapist becomes unlike anyone else the patient has ever met.

The issue then becomes one of attempting to correct the habitual perceptual distortion. The proposition I am offering is that no amount of attention paid to the contents of thought can succeed in correcting the habitual tendency. If anything, it succeeds only in reinforcing the distorting process by suggesting that the contents of thought can provide an accurate yardstick for healing. The content of the fantasies is not important but the *fact* of fantasy formation is. The phenomenologist is not interested in actively pursuing the patient's associations or impulses concerning the therapist or how the therapist might have provoked the distortion; he is concerned with the patient's *reacting* to an encounter by seeking explanations and interpretations from elsewhere to account for the reaction.

In an article called "Love and the Psychotherapeutic Eros," (1962), C. Seguin makes an important statement about the nature of the therapeutic relationship. He first delimits what it should not be by enumerating the five most fundamental relationships that occur in everyday life, *none of which* is to stand as the foundation of the therapeutic relationship. They are parent/child; lover/lover; friend/friend; teacher/pupil; pastor/flock. All of these relationships are built out of *mutual needs* and election to the particular status enacted in the relationship. They are all certain types of love relationships. While love is the fundamental soil from which all healing grows, none of the above relationships can promote healing because they are all based on turning the other into an object who can fulfill the subject's needs. To the extent that any therapeutic relationship is colored by any of the factors that determine any of the five basic relationships, the possibility for successful healing is thereby diminished. As Seguin points out:

> Another characteristic of the psychotherapeutic Eros is that it cannot be destroyed. Any of the other forms of love is easily annulled by one of the partners. Unfaithfulness will destroy the relationship between lovers, disbelief will break the one of the pastor with the follower, rebellion will estrange father and son, unsharing will part friends, independence will separate teacher and pupil, aggressiveness will kill any form of normal love, but none is able to deter the psychotherapeutic Eros. The patient may show all kinds of negative feelings, but they will not impair the therapist's love. They may even increase it, being, as they generally are, a demonstration of how much that love is needed. There is, however, one way which makes psychotherapeutic Eros to disappear as such: its transformation into any of the other forms of love. (p. 189)

I would like to add that a good psychotherapist is one who needs nothing from the patient. The person who needs any of the other "loves" is prone to using the patient to fill an emotional vacuum and thus, losing his center, would disqualify himself as a genuine psychotherapist.

What then constitutes successful therapeutic contact? The answer is complex; in general, as Seguin implies, it demands much more selflessness on the part of the therapist than is now required in most psychotherapeutic endeavors.

Within the therapeutic profession, there is much concern about the inability to provide significant amelioration of the world's mental suffering. Medard Boss, among others, has suggested that using logic-based therapy to treat suffering in fact exacerbates the problem. Not only is linear logic inadequate to deal with man's complete experience, but also, by refusing to recognize anything nonrational as genuine, organized psychology promotes the very illness it attempts to cure by cutting the patient off from the other experiences that constitute his world. The patient feels forced to conform to the idea of linear logic as the only reality, and must therefore reject himself. This misunderstanding by organized psychology has led to the dehumanization of therapeutics and the training of "health engineers" (Boss, 1963, 1979) who make the dehumanizing process more efficient.

In true healing, one must struggle with needs and their influence on therapeutic movement. What are the mutual needs of therapist and patient and what are the consequences for both partners? Consider the very terms, *therapist* and *patient,* which immediately structure a hierarchy between the two replete with images of power, dependence, and needs no matter how aware we are of the inadequacy of words to encompass the complexities they denote (Fabrega, 1976).[1] These labels grow out of the need of the therapist to be the expert and the patient to be helped.

When an individual begins to experience mental pain and finds he cannot "work it out" on his own, he goes to a therapist for help. Social conditioning has taught him that a trained expert will fix his problems for him. The trained expert has also been conditioned to see the patient as needing something done for him. Because of the prevailing reliance on linear thought as the only criterion to measure reality, the patient thinks he is inadequate, and the therapist has an entire theory of categories ("pathology," "schizophrenia," "neurosis") and forms of relationships ("transference," "anonymity of the therapist") to apply to the patient to prove this.

The result is the fostering of a distance between the two, where one is observer the other is observed, thus making for an unbridgeable chasm. The two are viewed as different in kind rather than different in level of development. The young musician goes to the piano teacher expecting help in his own training. He knows that his own practice with the instrument is what will make him a better pianist, not what the teacher will do for him. The teacher may show him new ways of fingering or suggest a different coloration, but he does not perceive the student as different in kind from himself, but rather at a different developmental stage. But the patient more often goes to the therapist unaware that growth will come out of his own resources; he expects to be done to and for. And the therapist with credentials on the door, and psychological nomenclature in mind, cooperates in this misconception by agreeing with the patient.

This is the attitude that the terms convey. The therapist is reassured by his label that he is different from the patient, whose label reinforces his self image as weak, inadequate, helpless, victimized.

Because there is tacit agreement that therapist and patient are different in kind, the patient, who needs help, feels inferior to the other. He wants to become not fully himself but more like the therapist. For his part the therapist feels superior and fails to recognize that his own needs and own behavior in fact affect the patient's behavior. The therapist has become a therapist because he needs to feel expert, needs to feel helpful, needs to feel he can relieve suffering, and the patient may often respond to these needs by trying to comply with the therapist's demands by remaining dependent and helpless.

Both participants have become objects of need and are seen by the other in terms of the image that will fulfill the need. Each has meaning for the other only if he fulfills his need. For true healing to occur, the therapist must guard against this attitude. In actuality, there is no transference or countertransference. Each person comes with his own image-making tendency, his own moral and ethical values, his own special conditioning. What is important is that the perceptual distortion and image-making habit on the part of both participants be recognized consistently and conscientiously. This persistent effort is required so that the needs do not distort the true being together of the partners in the therapeutic endeavor.

Most patients' experiences in life have been with people who inhibit their immediate contact with their emotions. Instead they are prompted to feel anxious when their attempts to focus on their own experience are met with a critical response. If, however, the therapist is able to accept the patient as he is, as genuine and real, he will be able to stay with the patient's experience of anxiety. The patient in turn will accept the therapist as being without precedent, someone unlike the others in his life, and he will not heap his habitual distortions on the therapist. But if the therapist's attitude mirrors that of the significant people in the patient's life and reinforces social conditioning, nothing can be gained in the therapeutic experience. The therapist then becomes an object of need, met with by old perceptual habits. During this distorting perceptual experience never does the patient mistake the therapist for anyone else; however he does see the therapist as an image of someone who will or will not fulfill his needs, similar to an important person in his life. Someone wants something, whether it be abstract or concrete, love or supper. He goes to another to fulfill his desire and the other responds in his own fashion. Up to this point, action is freely and consciously chosen. There is no issue of "unconscious" forces. There is no so-called determinism at play here. All movements toward what is encountered in the world are freely chosen.

The individual who responds does so by *his* freely chosen action. Depending on what this response is, that is, if the latter does or does not fulfill the first person's need (most often, in clinical situations we see the latter as a source of frustration) the first person goes a step further. He tries to shape the response to his action. He reacts by attempting to shape and control the other's response to conform to his need. This step accounts for a great deal of human misery and suffering.

A woman wants a man's attention. She is attentive and affectionate but he ignores her and instead turns on the television set. Since he has not fulfilled her need, she compounds her efforts to "get him" to pay attention. He still does not respond. She becomes increasingly frustrated and annoyed. An argument will very likely ensue. She is dependent on his response to fulfill her need. When that response is not forthcoming, she tries to shape or control his response to her but in fact, she is controlled and shaped herself. Why? Because his response or lack thereof dictates her next move, thought, or feeling, leaving her unfree and thereby controlled by him. Each of us could multiply this example by the dozens. This attempt to shape the other's response to fulfill one's own need is one of the core difficulties in the development of emotional problems. Such reaction extends the event in time and turns it from an emotional situation (something of the moment) to a feeling situation (something that has duration); it becomes an entity (a state), gives rise to memory, and tends thereby to evoke habitual painful experiences.

Habitual reacting is reflexive, not freely chosen, and has come to be designated as "unconscious". One reacts because the response to one's action did or did not satisfy one's need. Whichever of the two occurs is essentially irrelevant, except that more mental pain is experienced when the need is not fulfilled, and the frantic attempts that ensue to shape the response to fulfill that need are almost always unsuccessful. It is only at this point of trying to shape the response that most psychological clinical theory and description have their starting point (Fig. 7.1).

THE THERAPEUTIC RELATIONSHIP 189

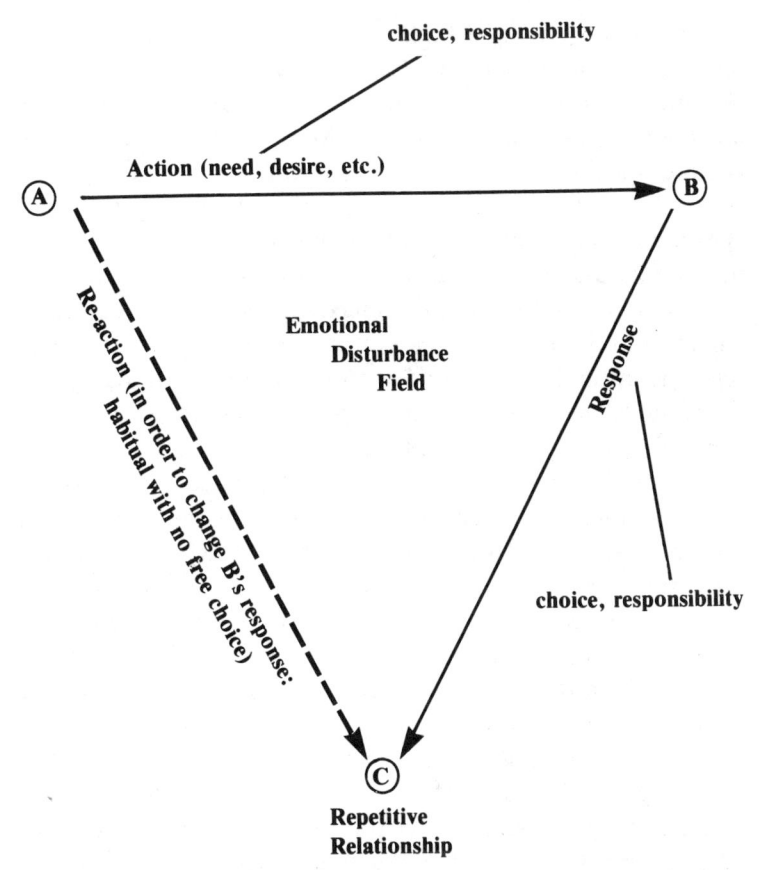

choice, responsibility

Action (need, desire, etc.)

(A) ──────────────► (B)

Re-action (in order to change B's response: habitual with no free choice)

Emotional Disturbance Field

Response

choice, responsibility

(C)

Repetitive Relationship

A acts with need or desire toward B. B responds. So far A has choice and responsibility for his act. Likewise, B has choice and responsibility for his response. If B's response does or does not satisfy A's need or desire and A's very next thought, feeling, or behavior, is directed by what B does or does not do in regard to that desire, then the stage is set for the development of what can be called the field of emotional disturbance. The emotional disturbance field is then governed by the attempt of A to change B's response (if desire is not fulfilled), or to maintain B's response (if desire is fulfilled). A at this point is completely unfree and is governed by his contingent dependency on B's response. A is controlled by B's response. A, in effect, is overstepping the limits of his responsibility and choice—which lies *squarely and only* on his own action—and is trying to claim responsibility for B's response by trying to control B's response. A, in this instance, is always *re*acting, i.e., acting again. Such reaction is always habitual, reflects no free choice, and is always doomed to failure.

Figure 7.1

All description and explanation of clinical phenomena are secondary, however, to the fundamental issue of having one recognize and understand that he is responsible only for, and has choice only over his own actions. To try to control or intrude upon someone else's freedom of action is an attempt that is doomed to failure (because, among other reasons, of the unaccountable variables in another's behavior), and falls outside the natural law of human conduct.

Freud based his clinical understanding of psychical determinism and human experience on the dichotomy of rationality versus irrationality. The fundamental nature of rationality and irrationality has never been elucidated; nevertheless Freud hoped that his therapy would help an "irrational," determined creature to become a more "rational," freely acting, volitional one. He summed this up in his oft-quoted phrase, "Where id was there shall ego be." However, the reality is that we are *fundamentally* freely-acting beings *to begin with* and that our freedom *precedes* our being determined. Our repetitive, monotonous, compulsive behavior occurs only *after* our action is initiated. In this connection, an important point to consider is that a human existence is defined by its actions. As humans, we have limitless possibilities, many of which are approached according to the dictates of our needs; these possibilities can be fulfilled or not according to the interplay of our genetic-biological predispositions and the influence of environmental forces.

Now it happens that there exist many more possibilities for fulfillment than one can realize at any one instant, so that in choosing any one a whole host of others are unfulfilled at that moment. Therefore, we live always in a state of having to take responsibility for what *we do not fulfill* as well as for what we do fulfill at every moment. That is, our fundamental relation to the world is guilt or *being in debt* to ourselves for what we do not do (Boss, 1963). After we react to the response of the other to our action, we begin to suffer from *feelings* of guilt—the aftermath of our anger, rage, frustration, and despair at not being able to control another's actions. (Those who can control other people's actions usually do not experience mental pain or feelings of guilt in connection with the fulfillment of need[s].) The essential point is that we *choose* our action or nonaction. *So, the order of human functioning is freedom, or freedom of will, followed by determinism, the reverse of Freud's perception.* Simply put, determinism belongs in the realm of mechanical action that obtains once an event is initiated. Will is the initiator of an event, responding as it does to formal cause (our potentials) and final cause (our purpose).

This perspective on human behavior may be of therapeutic benefit. By assuming that free choice precedes "psychic conflict," the therapist starts out by accepting the individual's fundamental freedom, a freedom the therapist shares. The therapist no longer needs to dissociate himself from his patient in order not to share his "aberration." The primary focus then becomes the acceptance and carrying out of action in accordance with those potentials that present themselves to us. Failure to act—to exert will—sets in motion all the conflicts of mental life. When I turn away from meeting something or someone that calls to me in the openness that is my human existence, I am beset by guilt. When someone calls upon or reminds me that I have not accepted my responsibilities toward that which I have turned from, then I might experience anger, resentment, or guilt toward the other as well as toward myself. I then might act to express this anger while engendering further feelings of guilt in myself. One emotional response begets another, and it is only this begetting that can be explained adequately along deterministic lines.

Nevertheless, the fact remains that prior to the emotional turmoil, there occurred some action for which I had to assume responsibility; responsibility not only for what I knew I had to do, but also for those potentials that would remain unfulfilled at that moment.

If my rejection of action is compulsive, that is, if I am enslaved in an habitual mode of behavior toward what addresses me from out there, this behavior is usually nonproductive and painful because I deal not with what is real but with my image of what is real as constructed in the past. I am no longer aware of my freedom to choose my action. The cause of my restricted behavior lies not in *what* happened to me in the past but in *how* my past has influenced my perception of the present.

I am born with certain possibilities into an environment that will permit or prevent their unfolding. My parents and other immediate family are the personifications of the environment that most directly determines whether the possibilities will grow or not. As I move into the world and potentials become more available to me, my perceptual responsiveness may become more distorted, depending on my past. If I perceive a situation as being similar to one in my past, I predict the response of the other and act accordingly. This means that I am aware of, and respond to, whomever enters my perceptual field. I do not mistake him for someone else. But my conditioning and force of habit lived as perceptual distortion restricts my range of responses, which are usually mechanical and tend to make an object out of whomever I am with. This means that new people become interchangeable with old ones when they behave in some way that elicits this repetitive response. I try to respond to whatever is present, but my perceptual distortion does not allow me to place the new person in the proper context. I know perfectly well that this individual is *not* my father or my mother; I do respond to him *as he is,* but my attitude is conditioned by how I have responded to someone else's sort of fatherliness or motherliness or authoritarianism, which I now perceive to be recurring. Although I know that a genuine other is in the immediate present, my preconceptions lock me into repetition so that I am unable to be truly with the other. My perception is attached to my preconception and one influences the other.[2]

From the outset the therapist encounters the patient with these sorts of perceptual distortions which can be triggered by the behavior of the patient. He is by no means a *tabula rasa,* nor is he ever neutral in the face of whatever he perceives to be an infringement of his value system. For example, by calling someone "my patient", the therapist is disposed to act mechanically and possessively toward him, treating him as his own object of need now that the labels have been fixed.

The difficulty arises by using the possessive "my." When someone possesses something, it belongs to him and he has a *vested interest* in what happens to the possession, regardless of whether it is animate or inanimate. Once the vested interest is developed, the object must fulfill the need that engendered the interest. And so the cycle, outlined by Figure 7.1 begins again.

A vested interest means a certain kind of caring about the other. I term this caring self-ish (without the usual, pejorative overtones). In contrast to this sort of caring is self-less caring in which the interest does not lie in what the other does nor in the values he holds, but rather in creating an environment in which the other may fulfill whatever he is able to. This caring is like that of the gardener, who does not presume to tamper with the petals of a flower but takes great care to provide the best conditions he can (proper soil, water, nutriment) to enable the flower to bloom and thrive. He does his work for the sake of the flower.

As Seguin has written:

> ... now we come to the positive part of the psychotherapeutic Eros and I want to emphasize, from the beginning, that it has to be a personal love for the patient or, better still, a love for the person of the patient. This I point out in order to eliminate the possibility of the love for the patient *in his condition of patient,* the idea of the doctor loving the sick *qua* sick being always present as a part of his professional duty. From the moment we see a man as a "sick man," we are placing ouselves automatically out of the real psychotherapeutic Eros. (p. 188–189)

In waking dream therapy, the instructor/advisor helps the explorer accept the reality of his own existence in the world. He reinforces three major truths: (1) what the patient finds belongs to him; (2) what the patient finds in imaginal existence is real and of a valence equal to that of waking life; and (3) his experience can be brought from the *there* of the imaginal world to enrich living in the *here* of the concrete world. The underlying attitude of the instructor/advisor to the explorer is trust in the explorer to discover on his own.

To undertake waking dream therapy, the explorer must have faith that the instructor knows his way through uncharted terrain. Faith is a requisite for healing. It is the enemy of scepticism and discrimination. As Abraham Heschel wrote in *God in Search of Man* (1955):

> Rabbi Mendel of Kotsk was told of a great saint who lived in his time and who claimed that during the seven days of the Feast of Booths his eyes would see Abraham, Isaac, Jacob, Joseph, Moses, Aaron, and David come to the booth. Said Rabbi Mendel: "I do not see the heavenly guests; I only have faith that they are present in the booth, and to have faith is greater than to see. (p. 118)

This, indeed, is the greatness of man: to be able to have faith. For faith is an act of freedom, of independence from our own limited faculties, whether of reason or sense perception. Since faith is the antipathy of scepticism, itself an offshoot of linear logical thinking, faith partakes of knowledge that precedes logical thinking. As Heschel again wisely puts it (1955):

> Only an extreme rationalist or solipsist would claim that knowledge is produced exclusively through the combination of concepts. Any genuine encounter with reality is an encounter with the unknown, is an intuition in which an awareness of the object is won, a rudimentary, *preconceptual* knowledge. Indeed, no object is truly known, unless it was first experienced in its unknown-ness.[author's emphasis] (p.115)

This preconceptual knowledge resides outside of time. For this reason, faith as part of that preconceptual knowing resides outside of time. To reside outside of time is to dwell in the present moment. Arthur Young in the *Geometry of Meaning* (1976) wrote thus:

> ... [F]aith, is the tendency to maintain a given credo without examination. Like the flywheel, it serves to maintain steady motion, carrying us through the vicissitudes of life.
> *Faith* and *inertia* (i.e., the scientific principle—my parenthesis) *are in the present. Faith is the projection we put upon the present situation.* [my emphasis] (p. 42)

The advisor promotes the explorer's faith by an attitude of tolerance and affection for his values and actions. In this way, he grants permission to the explorer to become. What develops in the explorer is a new relationship to another person that is divorced from his past experience.

This attitude must not be confused with permissiveness and misapplied charity, which are bound to lead the person toward whom these attitudes are directed to respond with scorn and abuse and an attempt to discredit the therapeutic endeavor.[3] Affection and open acceptance of the explorer is also different from the coldly detached, inquiringly objective analytic stance. The detached stance commonly affects the patient, who then becomes extremely intolerant toward himself or others, and it can lead to a breaking down of the spirit.

Too frequently in treatment the therapist reacts to the patient in a way that brings out the habitual, repetitive response in him, setting up an environment of mistrust. In contrast, I find that if the therapist does not dissimulate for purposes of fostering a supposedly clinical, nonintrusive setting, but is himself, he can establish a more viable environment for allowing the patient to contact his own healing potential. The example the therapist sets is very important for furthering therapeutic improvement.

The clinical situation promoting change in waking dream therapy is quite different from the one in the usual therapeutic relationship in which contingent, dependent, and causal factors are seen to be the agents of change. Dynamic therapy generally bases its leverage on the establishment of what is technically known as "transference," whereby all sorts of ideas about the meaningful personages in a patient's life are attributed to the person of the "neutral therapist." This perspective mirrors actual human relationships of the sort we are most accustomed to and which are based on dominance and submission, power and impotence, strength and weakness. "Dependence," "contingent," and "causal" are words that can be used interchangeably to describe how these relationships are established, and "determined" can be used as the general umbrella term under which all of these relationships exist in the dynamic framework.

The phenomenological approach holds that "transference" theory focuses on the wrong issue, the object of the distortion, rather than on the *fact* of the perceptual distortion itself. When therapy investigates the fact and amplitude of perceptual distortion, the patient can discover how habitual feelings color the perception of the immediate present and prevent access to more profound, genuine, autonomous emotions and thus to a genuine relationship to present concrete reality.

Another problem with "transference" is that it encourages the development of an habitual relationship in which the patient becomes dependent on the values the therapist subtly transmits to him, and he thereby loses the spontaneity that characterizes a creative relationship to life. In waking dream therapy, there is no impetus to end the relationship or "work it through;" the two participants maintain a lifetime connection (although not necessarily one of physical contiguity). But the advisor always encourages the explorer to try, to do, to live.

In waking dream therapy, dissolving the relationship is easier than in traditional therapy because the seeker learns for himself in a deeply felt way that he is the source and the initiator of his own experience. He generally becomes more insistent on carrying out what he must and concomitantly feels less need to continue his work with the advisor. This attitude of independent forging ahead must be encouraged so that the journeyer experiences his distinctiveness and difference from the advisor. If the advisor steps on the independence and freedom of the explorer, he risks being enmeshed by the explorer's attributing to him the responsibility for his own existence. Ideally, the relationship should be free from authority, possession, identification, dogma, the imposition of rules, values, or knowledge (Seguin, 1962, p. 187).

The instructor serves primarily to facilitate the explorer's internal process of changing his habitual perception of the world. He is a catalyst akin to those agents which accelerate chemical reactions without being consumed in the process. Once the process has begun to move in the desired direction, the catalyst is no longer required. So it is in the process of waking dream that the instructor withdraws from the process or is discarded by the explorer. The explorer's discovery of his internal instructor indicates that the external instructor is no longer needed. He can now call upon his internal instructor to signal the most salutary direction for his life. After the explorer meets his internal instructor, it is very important to point out that this instructor is there for him to find any time his presence is required; he should be made a living force in the person's life. Once this instructor is found, an immediate senses of faith and trust is established. If this faith is not forthcoming, the internal instructor is probably not genuine.

Since we are attempting to focus on living in the immediate moment, the traditional therapeutic paradigm is modified. The explorer is *literally* exploring his inner life and is dependent on his own capacity and will. He comes to see the "what" of his life (potentials and possibilities) and the "how" of his existence (the action he can take to fulfill those possibilities), rather than being preoccupied with the "why" of his life. The recognition of the what and how of life permits him to live more rationally. He becomes more in touch with the intrinsic harmony and connectedness of his life. His images are the language of his emotions. He begins to create new images—new emotions which then alter his habitual world image, built up of accretions of images since childhood. In this paradigm the advisor does not represent a figure from the past or present who triggers psychodyamic defenses related to the past and present. He is the catalyst in the process whereby imagination becomes a synthesizer of all modes of mental activity. Imagination becomes the agent for change and transformation.

After waking dream therapy has been completed the explorer still has access to all that he has discovered during his exploration. He can continue to do short exercises—they should take no more than one or two minutes from induction to completed eduction—in the morning before starting the day. They should come from the actual work accomplished in waking dream therapy and should bear on the continuation of some important aspect of his development elicited in waking dream. He may experience variations of the original event, and these should be welcomed. The daily exercise should follow exactly the stages in the original work: the induced relaxation, the journey, the return. *An individual is not to conduct his own waking dream* UNLESS he has found an internal instructor in his original work whom he can call upon by himself to escort him on an imaginal voyage.

One woman (case #103) experienced an enormous creative surge and growth during a waking dream journey. She began to sing, dance, and paint with great intensity and joy in her work. At one point in her journeys, she met Beethoven in a large room. He was seated at the piano, and she paid close attention to the music and his playing. Following this meeting she came to a special room in a house in the country, where she began to sing with a full throated intensity, seeing the sound emerge as a brilliant multicolored burst. In the days immediately following this exercise, she began to compose music and lyrics.

She continued to do the multicolored singing exercise every morning thereafter. In the two-year period since the conclusion of this work, she continued to do this exercise each morning and has continued to compose music. Her daily contact with a creative impulse has altered her attitude toward the external world. She had previously been characteristically downcast but now began to approach the day with a feeling of hope and purpose.

Another instance of someone continuing exercises after completion of treatment is that of a man who discovered great energy and life in a garden situated in a valley. In this garden, he found a golden eagle, a long golden staff, and clear water on which floated lotus pads, which each contained a black pearl. Following his work, he continued to go to his garden every morning to cleanse himself at the water's edge; he often rode on the eagle, and explored the garden with his staff. The daily exercise brought increased energy. Before, this man had routinely practiced psychotherapy; afterwards, he explored new methods, began to write about his findings, and ran a large clinic. All of these activities he attributed to the tapping of his creative resources during and after waking dream therapy.

The daily exercises begin while the explorer is in treatment so that he can accustom himself to the practice of this early morning activity. They are integrated directly into the fabric of the treatment, either before, during, or at the close of the session. The short exercise brings with it a positive attitude toward the day and usually molds the course of the day itself in a positive direction. The overall effect of waking dream work tends to infuse people with a feeling of hope.

Notes

1. I have tried to avoid this situation by substituting what I feel to be less charged terms: instructor/advisor for "therapist," and explorer (or journerer, voyager, searcher) for "patient."
2. Those called "schizoid," "borderline," and "schizophrenic" are prepared to encounter the people they meet as objects of need or fear to a much greater degree than that which obtains for the so-called "neurotic" or even "normal" individual.

3. For a most complete discussion of this subject, see *Tsedek* by Henri Baruk (New York: Swan House, 1972). Dr. Baruk has made outstanding contributions to an area of psychiatry he originated called *moral psychiatry,* based on the precepts laid down by biblical tenets.

Chapter 8

CONTINUING

If there are any fundamental ideas to draw upon out of the preceeding chapters, I would focus on three: unity, reality, becoming/being.

I have attempted to show that emotional life embraces a vast range of experiences, encompassing not only concrete reality but varieties of nonconcrete reality as well. In order to achieve a harmony, balance, and synthesis of relatedness in life, a unity of movement through these various dimensions needs to be established. This requires an unbiased, unpreconceived, and unprejudiced attitude to all possibilities of experience in order to offset the disunity engendered by reflexive intolerance toward the other dimensions by our habitual movement of thought. With an accepting attitude, we can enjoy the different realms of existence and profit from their influence on our everyday, concrete waking existence. It can be enriching to experience the merging of such realms while at the same time recognizing the distinctions between them. This process is a function of unity, which in itself is ultimately a movement of freedom. We can observe the opening into the domain of freedom in those with whom we work when both of us begin to notice the unity occurring between waking life, dream life, and waking dream life. When this unity occurs, we acknowledge as well our enlarged understanding of reality. When our perspective is informed by the experience of waking dream, we can no longer disregard the fact that *we exist in levels of reality and that these levels are real, i.e., places in which we exist*. They are not "projections" from an encapsulated psyche but rather are places that address us from out there—from somewhere in holographic space. The images that we encounter in imaginal work are concretizations of those realms. They disclose the life of the imagination and serve to awaken us to an inner life hidden behind the concrete world of everyday existence.

The movement of unity leads to valuable changes in the individual. One is that a person becomes less prejudiced toward himself and what he contacts within experience. He comes to accept the genuineness of what he actively engages in and becomes, thereby, less fragmented, feels more whole, and views himself as more authentic. His feelings of self-worth increase concomitantly. As waking dream life is granted its function to enrich and inform waking life, he begins to experience a greater freedom in his existence with a broadening of creative expression.

The effect of the movement of unity is not an automatic one that springs from the realizations incurred by the waking dream experience. The explorer must sustain the movement with continuing efforts until unity itself becomes a habit. When the person becomes aware of the importance of establishing the link between realms of reality, there is an imperative to carry out the unmanifest in the manifest. If this is not fulfilled, the person bears the burden of not living as fully as he knows he could. Shortchanging oneself creates guilt and suffering. The individual is always free not to carry out what is learned, but as in life when undertaking any venture, there is always a price to pay for doing or not doing. *The choice is always ours.*

Another change growing out of the movement toward unity is the experience of the possibility of freedom. By freedom I mean becoming aware of the presence and value of acausality within the cause and effect deterministic existence.

The events of the imaginal sphere do not obey the rules of ordinary logic. During the imaginal event, *only description* of the location and happenings is called for. There is no attempt at understanding, analyzing, interpreting, or theorizing. That is, thought as a movement of defining existence is discouraged and does not occur naturally in the spatial realm.

This reversing of our custom of interpreting what we encounter contains the healing possibility. Healing is achieving wholeness, and healing apparently is to be found outside of the contents of our linear thought process. In imaginal travel, we become at one with the movement of life and the natural rhythm of the flow of existence. By becoming movement, we participate in the fundamental spatiality that underlies our concrete human existence. Concrete existence obeys the laws of cause and effect, while the human nonconcrete existence obeys laws that are acausal and nondeterministic.

That is, when we exist beyond our physicality, as happens in dreams or waking dreams, we recognize the synchronicity rather than the sequentiality of human behavior. We recognize the simultaneity of life experience—how we can be *here* and *there* at the same instant. This recognition allows us to realize the sense of Aristotle's four-cause proposition. Not only do we function according to material and efficient causality, which applies strictly to the quantitative function of human existence, but also according to formal and final causality, the more qualitative aspect of human existence. By considering ourselves to be a blueprint of the universe analogous to Aristotle's formal cause—the microcosm of the macrocosm, and as such ideally limitless—we can begin to broaden the relevance of causality to human existence.

As we do this, it becomes clear that we attempt to carry out the design, to reproduce the macrocosm in our microcosm with the equipment at hand, namely, the human body. Once we begin to see this connection, i.e., stay with it and follow it through, the fourth of Aristotle's causes becomes apparent and meaningful. The fourth cause is *final*, i.e., our purpose for existing as a human form for the short span allotted to us on earth. If we make the effort to fulfill the blueprint with the equipment given us, we gain enlightenment, or fulfillment of being. Some experience this fulfillment as "holy" or sacred or cosmic, or transcendent. Whatever it is called, it addresses itself to our being here for some purpose. Not everyone will agree that this purpose necessarily resides outside of materialism, nor goes any further than fulfilling our physical needs. Some may resist the notion of purpose altogether, but this is difficult to comprehend, since most of human behavior is dictated by some idea of finality or goal. Otherwise there is no motive to act.

My experience with waking dream, both personal and with patients and colleagues who have undergone waking dream work, and who, in turn, have used it with their patients, has led me to some recognition of purpose. This recognition leads to an understanding that our acts in the world are meaningful. That is, we come to see that all behavior has a ripple effect that influences others far beyond what is immediately observable in the action. We then become very careful of our conduct toward, and in, the world and its inhabitants. For instance, this ripple effect can be seen dramatically, concretely, albeit destructively, in the example of the company that pollutes a river with its waste products. This pollution will have an enormous ripple effect on untold numbers of people, not to mention the creatures who inhabit the river and its surroundings, and who depend on the ecologic balance of nature.

The recognition of purpose, or incorporation of formal and final causality into the understanding of human nature, helps us accept all potentials for existence as genuine. We become more tolerant, impartial, and unprejudiced. In the treating professions, such an attitude helps the therapist establish a healing environment of faith and trust. A sense of final cause helps the therapist overcome his trained skepticism, or what I call the "reflexive no," which immediately distances him from his patient and transforms the patient into a pathological case to be treated with often unnecessary prescriptions.

To know there is a final cause encourages the recognition of the bonds and similarities between all men, of their common interest and spirit. This works against the current atmosphere of divisiveness, dehumanization, and lack of sharing, an attitude we see heightened in people we are called upon to treat. Without final cause, the central focus of the individual is reduced to the personal "I", or ego, which can only conduce to greater disconnection from our essential unity with the rest of nature.

Waking dream facilitates a number of desirable outcomes. As clinical action, it is a catalyst in overcoming and changing habits. It aids in moving from the reflexive "no" to the reflexive "yes," from defensive, inhibited, repetitive, and compulsive behavior to a more naturally flowing, free, and creative life.

The action of waking dream is like that of myths and fairy tales, which depict the fulfillment of potentials not ordinarily available to limited human beings. The laws governing these realms are different from those governing waking life. Julius Heuscher (1974) for one has pointed out that myths and fairy tales serve as palatable and accessibe instructions about the conduct of life.

Fairy tale protagonists are condensed, simplified characters with unusual powers. The stories accentuate the consequences and responsibilities of action, and the possibility of creating one's own existence. They stress the virtues of selflessness and the pitfalls of selfishness. And, as Cassirer (1944) puts it:

> Nothing has a definite, invariable static shape. By a sudden metamorphosis everything may be turned into everything. If there is any characteristic and outstanding feature of the mythical world, any law by which it is governed—it is this law of metamorphosis. (p. 81)

Ubiquitous metamorphosis allows constant hope

Unfortunately, adults are cut off from myths and fairy tales. Unfortunately as well, adults are unable to communicate to children the instructions set forth by myths and fairy tales. However, this can hardly be expected in a materialistic age which measures a man by the quantity of things he has accumulated, and believes that only what can be grasped by our senses in the world of material objects, is "real." It was set down several centuries ago that myths, fairy tales, and imaginings of various sorts, were unreal. So the connection between material and nonmaterial life was severed, and fairy tales, a form of the latter, have now become merely an amusement for children.

Waking dream helps to restore that lost connection, and what's more, restores it through an act of the individual himself. *He discovers and lives his own personal myth or fairy tale. He gives instruction to himself* to inform his manifest reality with what he learns in his nonmanifest reality.

Waking dream functions as the graft does in plastic surgery. Old unusable tissue is replaced by fresh, usable tissue—the success of the take depends on the effort of the receiver, who is his own donor, to carry out his own mandate. However, the person is always left free to fulfill or not to fulfill his potentials and possibilities for existence once they are recognized. Any bias against fulfillment comes from the concrete person acting here in the world against himself. Achieving fulfillment is a movement of unity which can be experienced as wholeness.

I am not trained in metaphysics, but my experience, as well as that of others who have engaged in waking dream, has led me to the conclusion that reality is a composite of many parts. There are concrete reality and nonconcrete realities; there are levels of reality, and reality of the present instant. There is nothing new in this (re)-discovery. It has been asserted and reported experientially by people of diverse cultures throughout the world at different times throughout recorded history. Western science and psychology until recently have been wed to the delimiting of reality as equivalent to "objective reality." "Objective reality" is that reality that can be measured by quantitative units and is always physical in nature. I have referred to this level as "concrete reality" throughout this book, because "objective" suggests an underlying preconceived philosophical attitude. "Concrete" in contrast refers to tangibility and is tied to sensory experience without bias. The part of our essential being that lives as a concrete existence will obey the laws of that spatial realm. These laws are causally derived and they constitute the ground of our being in the physical world.

Self-importance or egocentricity fights any movement toward unity or toward acknowledging levels of reality. If "I", or ego, am a self-contained, physically measurable entity, that is, if I exist apart from others, my limits defined by my physical body, then "I" remain forever and always supremely important, kowtowing to no one and acquiring all I can to support my self-importance, my egotism, my personal "I"-ness. At the same time, "I" remain forever dependent on the world as one giant object of need, yearning to satisfy my demands and to maintain my personal self-importance. In this framework it is extremely important to me not to allow this image to crumble because my whole world is constructed on it. To experience the possibility that my *personal self* is insignificant (actually a recognition desired by phenomenologists) fills me with fear of unfathomable proportion. Hence the necessity to persist in the culturally transmitted, habitual belief in the supremacy of duality and concrete reality.

Becoming refers to the carrying out of what beckons to us from the world as perceived possibilities. These possibilities clothe themselves in us and we live them either fully or deficiently within whatever particular way we choose to carry them out. From the perspective of phenomenology life constantly calls upon us to live out some possibility or other. Furthermore, each fulfillment calls forth the next one. Each action at its apex reaches a moment of inaction. This inaction immediately calls forth the next action, which calls forth inaction, and so on. A common example is walking: at the apogee of the step there is stoppage and the next step is then enacted. Another type of action observed in nature is cyclical. The moment of the flower's bloom announces its dying. Growth surges to its limit and the surcease of action occurs at the height of its flowering potential. The next movement is toward death, as it usually is in cyclical movements. So it is, too, when a human being is born. At the climax of the gestation period the infant bursts forth. This "blossom" begins to die at the moment it is announced to the world. This is a cyclical movement. The human being then begins his linear action that ultimately culminates in death, and return to the primordial elements, thus completing the cycle.

Once being is embodied in physicality, the laws that pertain to physical existence come into play. These laws are natural laws, givens that are independent of human volition. They demand that we, as part of nature, ceaselessly change, flow, grow, and die. All of these terms imply movement and action. So it is that from the waking dream perspective, all of these movements may be subsumed under the umbrella of becoming.

This holism[1] may be reflected concretely in the emergence, for example, of holistic medicine, which is based on the understanding that the imagination is part of human existence; also:

1. Imagination has a physiological correlate in the right brain
2. Its functional existence is recognized by other cultures. These cultures seem to be in touch with a phenomenon that enriches their life, and these cultures seem untroubled by many of the problems, notably narcissism and anomie, that plague us.

By discounting imagination, we are unbalanced in the fulfillment of our lives.

An acceptance of imagination leads to a holistic medicine which:

Epilogue

NOTES ON THE PHENOMENOLOGICAL MODE

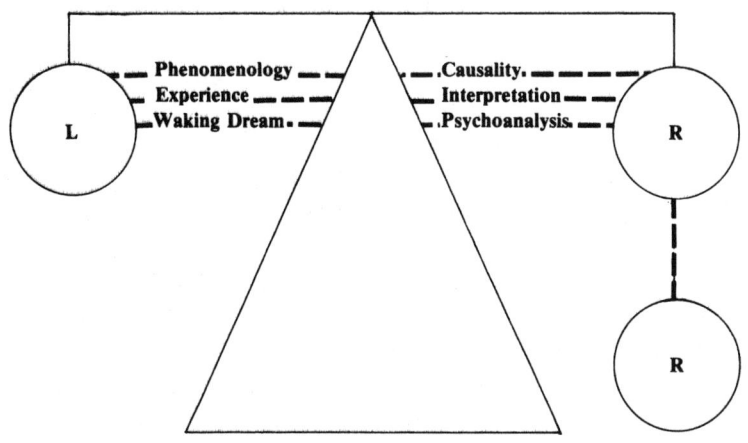

The necessity for balance is illustrated by this diagram. There is an overweightedness on the R side of the scale with respect to current psychotherapies (parted lines). The imbalance is addressed here by placing the polarities of the R scale terms on to the L scale. The introduction of these polarities on the L scale can help ensure a balanced and comprehensive therapeutic approach.

Figure E.1

The following polarities shown in Figure E.1 may help clarify the distinctions between the phenomenologically-based understanding of emotional life and that of traditional psychology.

211

Phenomenology———— Perception——Causality
Experience—————— Response——Interpretation
Waking Dream———— Therapy——Psychoanalysis

The initial perception in the overall relationship to the world (which includes inner experience) is either phenomenological or causal. Once perception is initiated, one is moved either to experience (act, do, live, create) some event or to interpret or give linear form to it. The therapeutic form that embodies deterministic causality and the interpretation of cause and effect is dynamic psychology. For 2000 years in western culture, linear thought (a movement *in* linear time) has been generally accepted as preparatory to action (a movement *out of* linear time). Phenomenology posits the reverse, that action enhances linear thinking: action permits new perceptions about the world.

Patients in treatment often say, "I don't know what to do." The traditional therapist usually accepts this statement at face value and tells the patient that he will come to know what to do by exploring the unknown in order to act rationally. On the other hand, the phenomenologist perspective takes a paradoxical stance toward the patient's remark, claiming from the outset that the person indeed knows what to do but that he *suffers from the inability to act, not the inability to know.* The fear, reluctance, or inhibition resides within the confrontation.

Therefore, in the phenomenological mode as it specifically applies to therapy, *the instructor/advisor encourages and supports action in order for one to be what one truly is.* In these instances the implication is always that an individual who does "not know what to do" is also "capable of knowing what to do" and is permitted to look at this side of things. This changes the focus from stasis to flow, from knowing to acting which is physically manifested. We sense from these journeys that we are able to gain access to those worlds within worlds—from waking reality, to fantasy reality, to dream reality, to imaginal reality. The movement to and from these worlds is the holomovement, the experiences encountered at each level a holographic phenomenon containing dimensionality but not volume (Fig.E.2).

The dream world is similar to the waking dream realm in its freedom from the time and space constraints of the concrete world. The dream, rather than being a product or creation of our brain is a phenomenological event, existing in a holographic spatial realm out *there,* apprehendable to human perception. It is a private world in and as which we live, that addresses itself

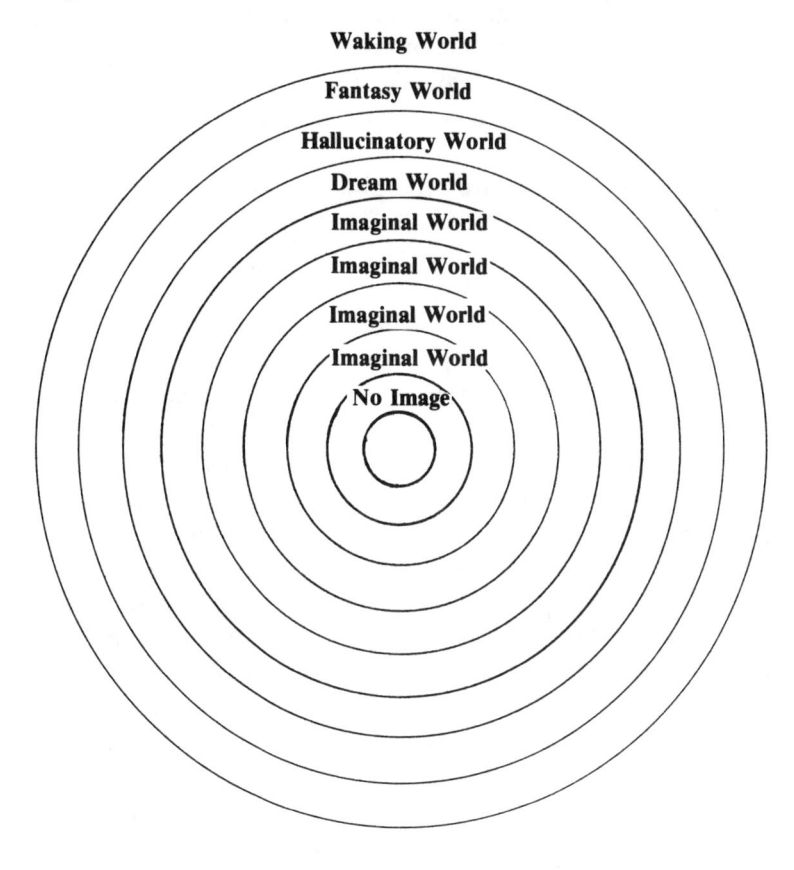

Waking World
Fantasy World
Hallucinatory World
Dream World
Imaginal World
Imaginal World
Imaginal World
Imaginal World
No Image

Figure E.2 The Holomovement. Worlds within Worlds.

to our sensory mechanisms. The meanings of dreams, however, while revelatory in their own way, are not as readily available as are those of waking dreams, where we can explore and expand.

Although both dreams and waking dream are experiential realms, the difference in the meanings they bear for us is related to the difference in the manner of entering the experience. We receive dreams passively by falling asleep, whereas we enter waking dreams actively by deliberately turning away from the concrete world through induced relaxation and we seek the imaginal realm with specific motives. It is the *active* approach to the imaginal realm that allows us to *translate* our experience there into action in the consensually shared world of concrete form.

In the dream, we are little aware of our determining the spatial directions or dimensions in which we move. There is little sense of freedom for the individual dreamer. There is also little sense of harmonization or equilibrium being established, which often leaves the dreamer feeling unresolved, unfinished, or unfulfilled after the dream. Or, the dreamer may become disharmonious by meeting and retreating from some frightening or otherwise disturbing entity in the dream.

In contrast, waking dream permits a movement experienced in and as freedom and harmonization. "Freedom happens as imaginative openness in determined states" (Scott, 1980). In night dreams, there is an awareness of *there;* in waking life, there is an awareness of *here;* in waking dream, there is *an awareness of both* occurring in the experiential moment. During waking dream the journeyer initiates his movement and does so with an intention to discover something of, for, or about himself. As he proceeds, he describes what occurs so that his *thereness* is immediately brought *here* and a link is forged between the two realms. No such luxury exists with regard to the night dream where the immediacy of the event is lost because the person has to awaken before he can recollect and describe the dream. In general, dreams are not usually reported to anyone and remain an internal event not brought into the perspective of the lived world.

Waking dream alerts us to the reality that the dream existence has its own spatial realm. *The action of waking dream enables us to move into or from this direct experience of the actual spatial process of dream existence.* That is to say, the dream becomes valued for its stated content.

The senses perceive content. However, the senses can also perceive nonmeasurable reality. Waking dream uses them to serve the imagination. The impact of waking dream on the individual helps him recognize the reality of spatial realms and helps him see the limits of rational thought.

This recognition can go a long way toward restoring imagination to its rightful place as a meaningful content in the chain of mental life, analagous to Freud's attempt at the turn of the century to return the dream to its rightful place in that chain. With the restoration of imagination and its qualitative, self-healing possibilities, the current psychophysiological discontinuity in western medicine can be made whole and continuous again.

The active forging together of inner and outer, "hereness" and "thereness," of connections between insubstantial matter and substantial matter, is the recognition and *experience* that we are more than what we define as our physicality. We experience a liberation from the sense of the individual personality. Man is, like light, both flow (wave) and entity (particle). The flow is our being. Becoming is a never-ending action without memory which is always engaged in the present. The particulate is the individual with its unique ego, memory, and history, and ultimately, stasis. With our given social conditioning, we tend to recognize only the particulate state and cling to it desperately to give ourselves security. Waking dream helps us to recognize the other aspect of our being: that the individual is a vehicle or conduit for experience to flow through. Waking dream gives form to the flow, and when that flow is translated into will, we can fulfill our possibilities completely.

Waking dream helps us aenesthetize the habits of everyday existence. This allows the development and exercise of new habits that can help us to live more harmoniously. One new action to help us live more within the rhythm of nature is to change our axis from the horizontal to the vertical, from the dimension of time to that of space.

Ordinarily we live in the horizontal realm, while the vertical surrounds us as a nonmanifest reality. We are not "unconscious" but rather "ignorant" of its existence. When the vertical axis is lived, our relationship to ordinary, everyday life temporarily ceases, only to resume again upon our return to the world of horizontality, which comprises the unfolding of time, sequential movement of thought and linear logic.

The movement of verticality can also be seen as moving from social relatedness on the horizontal axis to a more asocial state. In the vertical movement one is the solitary traveller seeking his own fulfillment; then one turns to the social context of human existence to participate more fully with others. Current psychological methods have generally concerned themselves with the entities, particularities, and contents that all make up our relationship to the everyday world lived in and as our five senses. These methods have concerned themselves with the movement of time, man's living of his past, present, and future as an historical event commonly lived as emotional valences ranging from joy to suffering (mostly the latter) in an habitual manner. Traditional psychology has concerned itself with a time-oriented approach to human suffering; it deals with the connections among the content of the movement of thought —the particles so to speak.

In contrast to the psychology of time, the phenomenology of space moves our appreciation of reality from a unidirectional, unidimensional one dominated by time to a broader and deeper appreciation of the totality of human possibilities of which time is but one. In this movement, we must also reconsider our designation of the term *psychology*. As a comprehensive term covering all aspects of human mental life, psychology implies two ideas: one is the strict definition, the other is the looser definition. Both definitions are problematical. The strict definition indicates the study of the psyche. The psyche is at best a hypothetical construct that is (1) unprovable; and (2) untestable, and (3) some "thing" possessed by a human being. By attributing the possession of a thing to a human being, one again falls into the habit of making man the sole and centrally important agent around which all events of nature crystallize. This study of what man possesses again accents the tendency to emphasize the thing, entity, or particulate-ness, and stasis of existence while drawing us away from the flow, stream, waveness, and change of our being. *From the outset we fail to recognize that we are both form and formless,* and that our task as humans is to become what we already are, a paradox of immense significance. For it is the resolution of this paradox, prominent among many others that define the ground of our being, that will allow us to move from becoming to being.

The looser definition of psychology, the idea of psychology as a study of human behavior, presents a fundamental difficulty that also inheres in the stricter definition. That difficulty is the equation of the study of man's behavior with the study of man. In truth, the two studies are different and are based on different approaches to the understanding of human existence. The study of human behavior is based on the belief that discovering something about the nature of man will tell us about his essence. A statement about man's nature says something about an attribute of man which may or may not have anything to do with man per se, that is, his essence. As Heidegger indicated, any statement about the nature of man is always an interpretation because it assumes an attribute. Language is always an interpretation of what is perceived. This idea emulates the principle of natural science, whereby, it is believed that the discovery of all the connective elements between a cause and the effect will lead to complete understanding of the effect. For example, natural science says that although it does not understand how a grain of wheat becomes a stalk of wheat, one day all the intermediate steps will be discovered. Likewise, although we do not understand what man is, we will get to know him by observing and cataloguing everything man displays. Each little piece, therefore, that is observed and recorded will fit into a composite picture that can finally be called man.

The problem is that this approach was developed for technology and the study of machines. To apply it to man is to assume that the characteristics of man are akin to those of machines. It is like trying to assess daytime by using attributes designed to study nighttime.

A person in emotional distress repeats habits that lead to closure and a stilling of growth. The unproductive repetition creates a sense of being chained or hopelessly bound up and brings with it a great deal of mental and often physical pain. The individual ordinarily does not have available the options to change the habitual patterns which are so reflexive that the behavior can be considered biological in nature.

In waking dream, the living through of an experience free of habitual tendencies releases a movement of more order, which permits a correction of habitual tendencies and allows a new direction in the person's development. There may also be a concomitant neurophysiological correlate: some neurophysiologists suggest that the transformational process effects the formation of new tracts in the brain.

If the imaginal existences are acknowledged and recognized as the genuine reality they are, then biological and physiological research in this area can broaden our perspective, just as physiological research helped illuminate dreaming. Such work has already begun to demonstrate differences between imaginal-like states and waking states. (Reyher, 1969; Singer, 1981).

In waking dream therapy, the fulfillment of possibilities is primary while verbal thought is put in its proper place of *describing rather than analyzing* action. Waking dream reveals that much of the disturbed person's life centers on inhibited action, such inhibition pushing him to see himself as always outside of the mainstream of human relatedness.

Waking dream clarifies what may be a fundamental principle of human existence alluded to by many psychological systems, which is that man lives in accordance with habitual tendencies that are conditioned by his biology and social influences to operate repetitively. These tendencies can for convenience be classified as positive and negative. The negative tendencies are essentially defensive and prevent our living in a natural rhythm, one that is a possibility if all of the positive tendencies or habits are encouraged. By living the negative repetitive tendencies inherited from childhood, we subordinate ourselves to what others have determined is an appropriate existence for us, and we are cut off from our freedom to live all that is potentially available.

I shall sum up what is most useful for an introduction to phenomenological therapy:

1. Waking dream work suggests the importance of an exploration of the phenomenology of space. This implies moving beyond the term *psychology,* which is understood as being applicable only to dealing with what is analyzed, not with what is synthesized. The phenomenology of space is concerned with movement, imagination, and description—a synthesis.
2. Principles and tools designed to study one set of phenomena cannot be used to study an entirely different set of phenomena. To do so is scientifically unsound and leads to rigidity and closed-mindedness.
3. The investigations of waking dream: (a) bring into focus the importance of right cerebral hemispheric functioning, and (b) can help to promote a harmoni-

zation of left and right cerebral hemispheric functioning.
4. My personal and clinical experience indicates that an awareness of formal and final causality is required in the successful treatment of man's emotional suffering. Without considering our potential and purpose for existence, and the presence of the transcendent, there can be no comprehensive approach to the treatment of emotional disturbance.
5. By paying attention to the importance of action, experience, and the fulfillment of possibilities, our focus is shifted from knowing through intellect to knowing through doing or living. Thus we move away from an overemphasis on the analyzing function to incorporating a synthesizing function—to the phenomenology of becoming and being.
6. By concentrating on the phenomenology of experience, we become connected much more vividly and intensely with the present and the lived moment of the present. We recognize that the past is completely observable in the present behavior but that we are not captured by the past.
7. Images are the concretizations of emotions. Imaginal work arouses our inner life and gives spontaneity and strength to our daily life. It prompts us to awaken to our life-giving and creative impulses and permits us to see that we can shape and create our experience and hence our existence.
8. The function of therapy changes when one becomes attuned to waking dream work. The effect of imaginal exploration is profound and long lasting, and the impact occurs quite soon after starting the work. The explorer recognizes his freedom to act and the importance of his own will in his own fulfillment. The advisor also recognizes the presence of freedom and

will and continuously develops an unprejudiced view of living and the necessity for experience. He constantly encourages the initiation of action and the movement of will. He has no stake in the "transference" relationship, knowing himself to be without precedent for the explorer, and he is always available to him.

9. Healing is the key to the cessation of imbalance and disharmony in emotional and relational life. Healing embraces the continuum from illness to health, a continuum that subsumes disease and cure. Healing also includes the religious and spiritual dimension, functions of the nonrational that, together with the rational, provide the wholeness and unity that inhere in the word *heal.* A complete therapy must include healing and thus becomes holistic.

10. The most significant, and perhaps revolutionary, finding (discovered by Mme. Colette Muscat and corroborated by my own experience) concerns the place of the five senses in finding our way at all levels of existence. The senses are the vehicles which take us through the gates into the imaginal existence, realms not apprehendable by our five senses in the world of concrete reality. Paradoxical as it sounds, the organs which habitually allow us to find the world of concrete reality also allow us to find those worlds of imaginal reality. This world of concrete reality is the actualization of the world of nonmaterial reality, which is the source of all form. When we move from the concrete reality to the imaginal, we move from concrete form to nonmaterial form. Such movement would not be possible without the use of the five senses.[1] The senses take us to and through the doors to our inner life. We go through them and are transported into imaginal realms.

NOTES

1. It is this understanding which corrects the common notion that when one enters an "altered state of consciousness" one takes leave of one's senses, or goes beyond one's senses. This is contrary to fact. The senses participate in all excursions into atemporal reality, for these events are biological as well as mental and emotional phenomena.

REFERENCES

Agus, J. *High priest of rebirth: the life, times, and thought of Abraham Isaac Kuk.* New York: Bloch, 1972.
Assagioli, R. *Psychosynthesis.* New York: Viking Press, 1965.
Atlan, H. The creativity and the reversibility of time. *Shefa Quarterly,* 1977, *I,* 40–54.
Bachelard, G. *The poetics of reverie.* Boston: Beacon Press, 1969.
Bachelard, G. *The poetics of space.* Boston: Beacon Press, 1969.
Baruk, H. *Tsedek.* Binghamton, N.Y.: Swan House, 1972.
Baynes, C., & Wilhelm, R. *The I Ching or book of changes.* New York: Bollingen Foundation, 1950.
Benoit, H. *The supreme doctrine.* New York: Viking Press, 1959.
Benoit, H. *Let go!* New York: Weiser, 1973.
Benson, H., & Wallace, R. K. The physiology of meditation. *Scientific American,* Feb., 1972, 84–90.
Bentov, I. *Stalking the wild pendulum.* New York: Dutton, 1977.
Blake, W. A vision of the last judgement. In G. Keynes (Ed.), *Blakes' complete writings.* London: Oxford University Press, 1966.
Bogen, J. The other side of the brain, II: an appositional mind. *Bulletin of the Los Angeles Neurological Society.* 1969, *34,* 135–162.
Bohm, D. *Wholeness and fragmentation.* Jerusalem: Van Leer Foundation, 1972.

Bohm, D. The enfolded order and consciousness. In G. Epstein (Ed.), *Studies in non-deterministic psychology.* New York: Human Sciences Press, 1980.
Boss, M. *The analysis of dreams.* New York: Philosophical Library, 1957.
Boss, M. *Daseinsanalysis and psychoanalysis.* New York: Basic Books, 1963.
Boss, M. *I dreamt last night.* New York: John Wiley, 1977.
Boss, M. *Existential foundations of medicine and psychology.* New York: Jason Aronson, 1979.
Cassirer, E. *An essay on man.* New Haven: Yale University Press, 1944.
Corbin, H. *Creative imagination in the sufism of Ibn-Arabi.* Princeton, N.J.: Princeton University Press, 1969 (Bollingen Foundation Series Vol. XCI, part 1).
Corbin, H. "Mundus imaginalis." *Spring* 1972, 1–19.
Corby, J., Roth, W., Zarcone, V., & Kopell, B. Psychophysiological correlates of the practice of tantric yoga meditation. *Archives of General Psychiatry,* 1978, *35,* 571–577.
Desoille, R. The directed daydream. San Francisco: Psychosynthesis Institute, 1966, *(Monograph #18).*
Eliade, M. *Myth of the eternal return or, cosmos and history.* Princeton, N.J.: Princeton University Press, 1954 [1965].
Eliade, M. *Images and symbols.* New York: Sheed and Ward, 1969.
Eliade, M. *Myth and reality.* New York: Harper & Row, 1975a.
Eliade, M. *Myths, dreams, and mysteries.* New York: Harper & Row, 1975b.
Epstein, G. A note on a semantic confusion in the 'fundamental rule' of psychoanalysis. *Journal of the Philadelphia Association for Psychoanalysis, 1976,* III, 54–61.
Epstein, P. *Kabbalah: the way of the Jewish mystic.* New York: Weiser, 1979.
Fabrega, H. Toward a theory of human disease. *Journal of Nervous and Mental Diseases,* 1976, *162,* 299–312.
Forman, M. B. (Ed.) *Letters of John Keats.* (4th ed.) London: Oxford University Press, 1952.
Freud, S. *The interpretation of dreams.* Vols. IV and V. *The complete psychological works of Sigmund Freud.* London: Hogarth Press, 1953 (58) [1900].
Galin, D. Implications for psychiatry of left and right cerebral specialization. *Archives of General Psychiatry* 1974, *31,* 572–583.
Gazzaniga, M. Review of the split brain. In M. C. Wittrock (Ed.), *The human brain.* Englewood Cliffs, N.J.: Prentice-Hall, 1977.
Gazzaniga, M., Bogen, J., & Sperry, R. Observations in visual perception after disconnection of the cerebral hemispheres in man. *Brain,* 1965, *88,* 221.
Govinda, L. *Foundations of Tibetan mysticism.* New York: Weiser, 1974.

Happich, C. Symbolic consciousness method, discussed by Kretschmer, W. in Assagioli, R. (Ed.), *Psychosynthesis.* New York: Viking Press, 1965, pp. 305–309.

Haule, S. (Ed.) *Color symbolism.* Zurich: Spring Publications, 1977.

Heidegger, M. *Being and time.* New York: Harper & Row, 1962.

Heidegger, M. *Poetry, language and thought.* New York: Harper & Row, 1971.

Heschel, A. *God in search of man.* New York: Farrar, Straus, & Giroux, 1955 (77).

Heuscher, J. *A psychiatric study of myths and fairytales.* Springfield, Ill.: Charles Thomas, 1974.

Hirai, T. *Psychophysiology of Zen.* Tokyo: Igaku Shoin, 1974.

Horowitz, M. *Image formation and cognition.* New York: Appleton, 1970.

Jung, C. G. *The collected works of C. G. Jung,* Vol. 16. Princeton, N.J.: Princeton University Press, 1954, p. 199.

Kaplan, E. K. Gaston Bachelard's philosophy of imagination. *Journal of Philosophy and Phenomenological Research,* 1972, *33,* 1–24.

Keats, J. Ode to a nightingale, in *The complete poems of Keats and Shelley.* New York: Random House (no date), p. 185.

Kernberg, O. *Borderline conditions and pathological narcicissm.* New York: Jason Aronson, 1975.

Kleitman, N. *Sleep and wakefulness.* Chicago: University of Chicago Press, 1963.

Kohut, H. *The analysis of the self.* New York: International Universities Press, 1971.

Kohut, H. *Restoration of the self.* New York: International Universities Press, 1977.

Kosbab, P. Imagery techniques in psychiatry. *Archives of General Psychiatry,* 1974, *31,* 282–290.

Kretschmer, W. Meditative techniques in psychotherapy in Assagioli, R. (Ed.), *Psychosynthesis.* New York: Viking Press, 1965, pp. 304–315.

Leuner, H. Guided affective imagery. *American Journal of Psychotherapy, 1969, 31,* 4–22.

Leuner, H. The role of imagery in psychotherapy, in Arieti, S. & Chrzanowski, G. (Eds.), *New dimensions in psychiatry.* New York: John Wiley, 1975.

de Lubicz, R. A. Schwaller. The intelligence of the heart: an outline of the symbolic method and its hieratic nature. *Parabola,* 1977, *II,* 18–27.

de Lubicz, R. A. Schwaller. *Symbol and the symbolic.* Brookline, Mass.: Autumn Press, 1978.

McMahon, C. The role of imagination in the disease process. *Psychological Medicine,* 1976, *6,* 179–184.

Mundy-Castle, A. C., & McKiever, B. L. The psychophysiological significance of the galvanic skin response. *Journal of Experimental Psychology* 1953, *45,* 15–24.

Pribram, K. *Languages of the brain.* Englewood Cliffs, N.J.: Prentice-Hall, 1971.

Pribram, K. Holographic memory. *Psychology Today,* 1979, 71–84.

Price, H. H. Survival and the idea of 'another world'. In Smythies, J. R. (Ed.), *Brain and mind.* London: Routledge & Kegan Paul, 1965.

Reyher, J. Electroencephalogram and rapid eye movements during free imagery and dream recall. *Journal of Abnormal Psychology,* 1969, *74,* 576–582.

Russell, G. (AE). *The candle of vision.* New Hyde Park: University Books, 1965.

Rychlak, J. *A philosophy of science for personality theory.* Boston: Houghton-Mifflin, 1968.

Scholem, G. *Major trends in Jewish mysticism.* New York: Schocken Books, 1941 (61).

Schrödinger, E. The spirit of science. In J. Campbell (Ed.), *Spirit and Nature: Papers from the Eranos Yearbooks.* Bollingen Series XXXI. Princeton, N.J.: Princeton University Press, 1954.

Scott, C. Freedom with darkness and light: a study of myth. In G. Epstein, (Ed). *Studies in non-deterministic psychology.* New York: Human Sciences Press, 1980.

Seguin, C. Love and the psychotherapeutic eros. *Acta Psychotherapetica et Psychosomatica,* 1962, *X,* 173–192.

Séjourné, L. *Burning water.* Berkeley, Ca.: Shambala, 1976.

Sheehan, P. (Ed). *The function and nature of imagery.* New York: Academic Press, 1972.

Singer, J. *Imagery and daydream methods in psychotherapy and behavior modification.* New York: Academic Press, 1974.

Singer, J. The psychotherapeutic implications of imagery. *The Academy Forum of The American Academy of Psychoanalysis,* 1978, *22,* 10, 15.

Singer, J., & Pope, K. *The stream of consciousness.* New York: Plenum Press, 1978.

Sperry, R. Lateral specialization of cerebral function in the surgically separated hemispheres. In McGuigan, F. (Ed). *The psychophysiology of thinking.* New York: Academic Press, 1973.

Stewart, K. Dream theory in Malaya. In Tart, C. (Ed). *Altered states of consciousness.* New York: John Wiley, 1969.

Ten Houten, W., & Kaplan, C. *Science and its mirror image.* New York: Harper & Row, 1973.

Watkins, M. *Waking dreams.* New York: Gordon and Breach, 1976.

Weaver, R. *The old wise woman.* New York: Putnam, 1973.
Wilber, K. *The spectrum of consciousness.* Wheaton: Theosophical Publications, 1977.
Young, A. *The geometry of meaning.* New York: Delacorte Press, 1976.

Index

Aboulafia, Abraham, 41
Aboulker-Muscat, Colette, 19, 221
Absolute matter, 97n
Abraham, 23
Acausality 29, 35, 152, 153
 (*See also* Non-determinism)
Acting out, 32
Action, 23, 154, 212
Actional trying, 32
Active imagination, 24, 45
Advisor, 23, 91, 95, 96n., 180
 (*see also* Instructor/advisor)
Akiba, Rabbi, 40–41
Altered states of consciousness, 59n.

Amulet, 14, 93
Ascent, 172–173, 177
 (*see also* Verticality)
Assagioli, Roberto, 44
Attention, 147
Axis mundi, 174
 (*see also* Eliade, M.)

Bachelard, Gaston, 149, 175
Balance, 28, 51, 211
Baruk, Henri, 200n.
Becoming, 98, 122, 207–209, 215
Being, 60n, 98, 208, 215
Benson, Herbert, 64
Blake, William, 16
Bogen, Joseph, 12

Bohm, David, 50, 150–151
Boss, Medard, 175, 185, 190
Brain, 46–49,
    and mind, 53
Brown, Dan, 96n.

Candle of Vision, 16
Cartesian thought, 13
    (*see also* Descartes, R.)
Cassirer, Ernst, 151, 205
Causality, 153
    and dependent-contingent thinking, 181–182
    final, 203–205
    formal, 203–204
Cave, 125, 126
Center, 174
Central axis, 170
Cerebral hemispheres, 49
    (*see also* Right cerebral hemisphere)
Cognitive imagination, 15
Color, 128–131, 145n.
Concrete reality, 37n.
    (*see also* Objective reality)
Consciousness, 53–54, 59n.
Contingent dependency, 132, 146n.
Corbin, Henry, 14, 15, 28, 30, 38, 39, 178n.
Corby, John, 65
Countertransference, 188

Daily imaginal exercises, 80
Descartes, Rene, 38
    (*see also* Cartesian thought)
Descent, 174
    (*see also* Verticality)
Desoille, Robert, 19, 41–42
    and Rêve Éviellé Dirige, 41–42
Determinism, 191
Drawing, 127
    (*see also* waking dreams notebook)
Dreams, 17, 18, 97n., 213
    and Senoi Indians, 27
    as realm of existence, 20
    in waking dream therapy, 132–140
    latent content, 17
    manifest content, 17
    vs. waking dream, 213–215
Dynamic psychology, 212

Eduction, 70ff.
EEG waves, 64, 65
Eliade, Mircea, 169, 174–175, 178n.
Emotion, 121
    (*see also* Images)
Empiricism, 37n.
Enlightenment, 205
Existence, realms of, 28, 30
Experience, 20
    and laws of existence, 34–35
    and normality, 35

and objective psychology, 35–36
and reality, 35
as psychology, 34
vs. linear thought, 34
vs. logic, 34
Explorer, 97n., 179–180, 199n.

Fabrega, Horacio, 185
Fairy tales, 205–206
Faith, 194–195
Fantasy, 13, 157–158
Feelings, 84
Five senses, 36, 60n., 63
  (*see also* Senses)
Four causes, 153
  (*see also* Causality)
Freedom, 190, 191, 202, 203
Free will vs. determinism, 191
Freud, Sigmund, 50–51, 154
  and clinical phenomena, 190
  and psychological theory, 151
  use of imagery, 24–25
Future, 33–34

Gabor, Denis, 47
Galin, David, 12, 46
Gazzaniga, Michael, 12, 49
Gestaltic perception, 14, 45, 46
Going, 83, 85

Going and returning, 23, 68ff.
Guided affective imagery, 43
  motifs, 43–44
  (*see also* Leuner, H.)
Guided exercise, 9, 16, 21, 23, 62, 117–122
  room cleaning, 118–119
  flower, 119
  garden, 120
Guilt, 190, 191

Habits, 218–219
Hallucinations, 54
Happich, Carl, 41, 42
Healing, 51, 81, 83, 89
Heidegger, Martin, 52, 217
Heisenberg, Werner, 60n.
Hemisphere functioning, 46
  (*see also* right cerebral hemisphere)
Here, 20, 159, 180, 181
Hereness, 133, 171, 215
Heschel, Abraham, 194
Heuscher, Julius, 205
Hirai, Tomio, 65
Holism, 208
Holistic, 13, 14
Holistic medicine, 13, 208–209
Hologram, 47–49
Holography, 47
Holomovement, 213
Hope, 9, 180
Horowitz, Mardi, 45–46

Human being, 53, 56
Hypnosis, 64, 65

I Ching, 39–40, 58n., 170
Images, 29, 84, 220
  (see also emotions)
Imaginal, 29, 40, 41, 157
  realm, 18, 36, 157
  world, 23
Imaginal activity, 18–19
Imagination, 11, 13, 14, 16–18, 49
  and holistic medicine, 208
  as faculty, 149
  as organ of perception, 149
  as spatial dimension, 149
  definition of, 38–39
  eastern use, 39 et seq.
  western use, 41 et seq.
Imaginative function, 14
Imaginative power, 15
Induced relaxation, 64–66, 214
Induction, 64ff., 147
Insight, 83
  and theory, 150
Instructor, 23, 81–83, 85–86, 96, 97n., 179, 197
Instructor/advisor, 93, 95, 180–182, 199n., 212
Intelligence of the heart, 14, 18
Intention, 63, 68, 83, 147

Internal instructor, 93–94, 197, 198
Interpretation, 24, 26, 82
  vs. translation, 154
Interpretation of Dreams, 11

Jacob's dream, 170
Journeyer, 146n.
  (*see also* Explorer)
Journeying
  and pilgrimage, 159
  example, 73–79
Judaism, 40
  and Kabbalah, 40–41
Jung, Carl. G., 24, 60n.
  and active imagination, 45

Kabbalah (*see* Judaism)
Keats, John, 15, 16
Kernberg, Otto, 56, 57
Knowing, 154–155
  as experience, 155
  as intellect, 155
Kohut, Heinz, 56
Kuk, Abraham I., Rabbi, 17

Left cerebral hemisphere, 49
Leuner, Hanscarl, 43–44
Lexical mode, 45, 131
Linear thought, 22
  as deterministic logic, 49
  connection to past, 33–34
  nature of, 33
Logical positivism, 37n.

INDEX

Magic, 145n.
Man, 217
McMahon, Carol, 13
Meaning, 152, 154
Medicine, 13
Meditation, 43, 64, 65
   viz. waking dream, 63
Meditational relaxation, 42
Memory, 116
Mendel of Kotsk, Rabbi, 194
Mind, 49, 53
Minor hemisphere, 50
   (*see also* Right cerebral hemisphere)
Motion, 22
Movement, 21, 145n., 175, 178n.
   directions of, 127–128
Mundus imaginalis, 14
   (*see also* Corbin, H.)
Myths, 205–206

Narcissism, 21, 52, 56, 57, 173, 174
Natural science, 32, 217–218
Neurophysiology, 218
Night dream (*see* Dream)
Nondeterminism, 27, 34, 147, 149
   vs. deterministic causality, 153
   (*see also* Acausality)
Nonlinear thinking, 51
Nonphysicality, 56
Nonrational, 27
   vs. rational, 26
Nonrational faculty, 17

"Ode To A Nightingale," 15–16
Ontic, 31, 32
Ontological reality, 14, 15, 19, 39
Ontological truth, 17
Oriental mode, 39

Paradox, 217
Patient, 36n.
   as explorer, 97n.
Perception, 22, 45, 212
Personal I, 52, 55, 56, 57
   and schizophrenia, 57
Phenomenological therapy, 219–221
Phenomenology, 18, 81, 116, 147, 156
   and creativity, 144
   and doing, 212
   and experience, 151, 220
   and knowing, 212
   and metaphor, 91
   and reality, 216
   and space, 98, 155, 216
   and transference, 196
   principle of, 31
Physical, 60n.
Physicality, 56
Physical activity, 97n.
Possibility(ies), 22, 153
Potential(s), 154

Preparation, 94–96, 159
Pribram, Karl, 47
Price, Harry, 15
Primary spatiality, 156
Principles, 95, 98
Processes of mentation, 27
Psyche, 217
Psychiatric classification, 54, 159, 183
Psychoanalysis, 50–51
  vs. religion, 51
Psychology, 217–218
  and Freud, 151
  and time, 216
  tenets of, 151
Psychology of time, 97, 216
Psychotherapy, 51–53
Psychotherapeutic eros, 185
  (see also Seguin, C.)

Qualitative existence, 21
Quantitative existence, 21

Reality, 57, 207
  abstract, 50, 58
  and egotism, 207
  and experience, 54
  and philosophical prejudice, 32
  aspects of, 20
  concrete, 54, 57
  enfolded, 50
  experiences of, 20
  levels of, 54, 55
  objective, 54
  viz. concrete, 60n.
  vs. concrete, 207
  unfolded, 50
Realms of existence (see Existence)
Relaxation state, 64, 65
Religion, 51
Responsibility, 181–182, 189, 191
Returning, 85–86
  (see also Going and returning)
Rêve Éviellé Dirigé, 41–42
  motifs of, 42
  (see also Desoille, R.)
Reversing, 90
Reversing habits, 87
Right cerebral hemisphere, 12, 14, 46, 49
Russell, George ("AE"), 16
Rychlak, Joseph, 26

Sacred, 40, 50, 174
Schizophrenia, 21, 57
Schwaller de Lubicz, R. A., 14, 131
Searcher (see Explorer)
Seeker (see Explorer)
Seguin, C. A., 184, 193, 197
Séjourné, Laurette, 14
Senoi Indians, 27
Senses, 49, 215, 221, 222n.
  (see also Five senses)
Short exercises, 198–199
Singer, Jerome, 45

Sign(s), 91, 92, 123–124, 152–153, 169
Space, 155–157
  directions in, 127
  phenomenology of, 155
Spatial realms, 84
Sperry, Robert, 12
Spiritual impulse, 176
Symbol, 151, 152, 169, 178n.
  and birth, 166–167
  and death, 166
  and movement, 166
  and semiotics, 161
  and transcendence, 161
  as bridging function, 163
  in psychology, 161
  vs. sign, 160–161
Synthesis, 32, 50

Talisman, 14, 92
Talmud, 60n.
Tantric Yoga, 65
Tendencies, 83
Theory, 150–151
Therapist, 19, 23, 36n.
  as instructor/advisor, 97n.
There, 21, 53, 159, 180, 213
Thereness, 133, 156, 214, 215
  and ascension, 176
Tibetan Buddhism
  and imagination, 40
Tibetan Buddhist
  psychology, 59n.
Time, 87, 156
  and entropy, 155
  and knowing, 155
  in linear thinking, 155
  in psychology, 155
Torah, 40
Transference, 82, 183, 187
  and phenomenology, 196
  in dynamic therapy, 196
Traveller (*see* Explorer)
Trial action, 32, 33

Unconscious, 61n., 154, 164
Unity, 201–206
  and acausality, 203
  and healing, 203
  and levels of reality, 202
  as freedom, 202–203

Vertical axis
  (*see* Verticality)
Verticality, 169–175, 177
  vs. horizontality, 216
Visual function, 12
Visual mode, 131
Visual phenomena, 16
Voice of instructor, 73
Voyager (*see* Explorer)

Waking dream, 12, 15, 16, 18–20, 47, 60n., 62, 73–79, 204–205, 214–215
  in traditional therapy, 129
  vs. dream, 133, 213–215
Waking dream notebook, 70–73

Waking dream therapy, 15
Waking dream voyage, 23
Waking life, 14, 17
Wallace, Robert (*See* Benson, H.)
Watkins, Mary, 15
Weaver, Rix, 24

White cape, 137, 146n.
Will, 89, 90, 147–149, 179
  in hypnosis, 64
  in waking dream, 64

Young, Arthur, 195

Case Index

#6, 100–102, 143
#7, 117
#10, 144
#14, 116, 120
#15, 79–81, 84–85
#18, 140
#23, 106–110
#30, 143
#34, 128
#37, 110–116
#41, 143
#42, 102–106, 172
#50, 87–88
#51, 176

#59, 91–92
#63, 130
#68, 145n.
#77, 125–126
#82, 133–139, 146n.
#86, 88–89, 140
#90, 90–91, 99–100, 167–168
#92, 127
#100, 146n.
#103, 198–199
#112, 119–120
#125, 123
#135, 171–172

$19.95

616.8914
E64
93874

WAKING DREAM THERAPY